Manifesto

Manifesto

THE REVOLUTIONARY SERMON ON THE MOUNT

GREG SIDDERS

Manifesto
© 2022 by Greg Sidders

All rights reserved. No part of this book may be used or reproduced in any manner whatsoever without the prior written permission of the author. The only exception is brief quotations in printed reviews.

ISBN 9798799889203

All Scripture quotations, unless otherwise indicated, are taken from the Holy Bible, New International Version®, NIV®. Copyright ©1973, 1978, 1984, 2011 by Biblica, Inc.™ Used by permission of Zondervan. All rights reserved worldwide. www.zondervan.com.

Scripture quotations marked (NLT) are taken from the Holy Bible, New Living Translation, copyright ©1996, 2004, 2015 by Tyndale House Foundation. Used by permission of Tyndale House Publishers, Carol Stream, Illinois 60188. All rights reserved.

Italics within Scripture quotations reflect the author's emphasis.

Cover design by Taggert Corn

To Steve
Proverbs 18:24

Contents

Manifesto 9
Pace 11
Poverty 12
Tears 15
Meekness 17
Hunger 20
Mercy 23
Purity 25
Peacemaking 27
Persecution 30
Reputation 32
Salt 34
Light 36
Rules 38
Law 41
Greatness 44
Righteousness 46
Anger 49
Reconciliation 51
Grudges 54
Adultery 57
Excision 59
Divorce 61
Swearing 64
Self-Defense 66
Litigation 69
Kindness 71
Generosity 73
Graciousness 76
Enemies 78
Perfection 81
Exhibitionism 83
Giving 85

Prayer 87
Superstition 89
Reverence 91
Kingdom 93
Provision 96
Forgiveness 98
Temptation 100
Bitterness 102
Fasting 105
Investments 107
Treasure 109
Vision 111
Money 113
Worry 115
Priorities 118
Compartmen-
talization 120
Today 122
Judging 124
Recompense 126
Modeling 129
Humility 131
Discernment 133
Expectation 135
Fatherhood 137
Love 140
Salvation 142
Fruit 144
Lordship 146
Obedience 148
Miracles 150
Foundation 152
Debrief 155

Manifesto

IT WAS THE MOST REVOLUTIONARY SPEECH ever delivered.

No one knows exactly how long Jesus spoke. Matthew was able to recall and record 15 minutes of it, give or take, and Luke's interviews yielded just 5. But never have so few words had such immeasurable impact.

It wasn't the structure of the Sermon on the Mount that accounted for its greatness, for there was no single idea repeated with the cadence of hammer and nail. In fact, it is a wonder that anyone retains more than a fraction of what he said, so vast was the acreage of ethics he covered with such brevity. Listening to him must have felt like being served a full-course meal on a conveyor belt. One bite and it was on to the next subject. Yet each morsel was heavenly, worth savoring. Only when the sermon was written down did it become possible to fully ingest.

No, not fully. We have been gaping at it for two millennia and it still feels holy, impenetrable. The words we grasp, but the wisdom is deeper than we can plumb. No matter how slowly we read, or how long we ponder, we are out of our depth. Every reader is a novice, every reading elementary.

Imagine being there. Who among the thousands that sat in the natural amphitheater of that grassy plateau knew that Jesus was about to describe with such clarity and specificity the kind of life God created us to live? They expected parables, but instead they got a manifesto. To hear those words from the lips of Christ himself was an invaluable blessing. But Matthew, who was there, and Luke, who felt the power of Christ's words even as he heard them second-hand, wanted those who could not be there to at least read them, because never before had it been more clear how to do the will of God on earth as it is done in heaven.

But do we have ears to hear? The living word has been handed down to us in flat black type, pressed onto plain white paper, hidden in a leather-jacketed book that has no natural appeal to busy consumers with endless options. Our pace and our attention span blur the treasure that we race past on our way to the newest hollow attraction.

Rare, therefore, are those in today's world who are willing, indeed able, to quiet their soul long enough to relish this treasure. Rarer still are those who assimilate it, putting Christ's words into practice. But all who do, however erratically, find, in a world of sinking sand, that elusive bedrock upon which the life we want—and the life God wants for us—can be built.

Pace

THE CHAPTERS YOU ARE ABOUT TO READ are brief enough to grind out several in each sitting. But they were written to be read in daily increments so that your mind and heart have the time and space to genuinely absorb each sentence of the Sermon on the Mount. The questions at the end of each chapter are also intended to be answered slowly and prayerfully, connecting truth with life.

The benefit you derive from this book may well come down to pace. The slower, the better.

MATTHEW 5:3; LUKE 6:20, 24

LISTENING TO JESUS is like looking at the sun. Most of us can't do it for long, and the intensity must be reduced with darkened lenses. This is why we so often conclude that Jesus could not possibly have meant what he clearly said. We can't handle the truth unfiltered.

And then someone comes along who has the rare ability to take Jesus at his word, and we are undone.

Matthew the former tax collector was in the crowd when Jesus delivered the Sermon on the Mount. He heard the Lord's voice clearly, and yet when the time came to write down, from memory, what Jesus said about poverty, his mind had long since spiritualized it. "Blessed are the poor in spirit," he wrote, "for theirs is the kingdom of heaven" (Matthew 5:3). It's not that Matthew was inaccurate. It is true that the kingdom belongs to those who know they are morally bankrupt in the eyes of a flawless God. Only onto blank resumes does the blood of Christ drip, making holy those who know they are doomed without grace. The Spirit of God revealed that priceless truth to Matthew and inspired him to write it down.

But it is unlikely that Jesus said it exactly that way. Others who were there remembered that Christ's exact words were, "Blessed are you who are poor, for yours is the kingdom of

God"—and that, in fact, he went on to say, "Woe to you who are rich, for you have already received your comfort." When Luke confirmed the accuracy of the quote, he had the gall to include it in his biography of Jesus without alteration. There it is, in the 6th chapter of his gospel, verses 20 and 24, blinding and appalling.

Was Jesus really talking about net worth when he said that poverty is a blessing and wealth a woe? Yes, he was, and if you can't think about it for more than 10 seconds without looking for a loophole or hoping that it means something else in the original Greek, join the club. Jesus was turning conventional wisdom—not to mention orthodox theology—upside down. After all, the Hebrew scriptures said that wealth is a blessing from the Lord (Proverbs 10:22). But Jesus came and said, well, the opposite. "Blessed are you who are poor."

We cannot help but look away. We memorize Matthew's version, not Luke's, and we reason that there is no need to take Jesus literally. Just be poor in spirit, because the issue is not financial. Never mind that, if we keep reading through Luke, we'll have to shield our eyes again and again, because for some reason he was a collector of the most radical statements Jesus ever made about money. "Give to everyone who asks you, and if anyone takes what belongs to you, do not demand it back" (Luke 6:30). "Sell your possessions and give to the poor" (Luke 12:33). "Those of you who do not give up everything you have cannot be my disciples" (Luke 14:33). "You cannot serve both God and money" (Luke 16:13).

We may be able to justify the value we place on wealth, but let's at least acknowledge that Jesus said poverty is preferable.

How is the Spirit of Jesus leading you to decrease your wealth? If you don't know, are you willing to ask him?

Tears

MATTHEW 5:4; LUKE 6:21, 25

SADNESS IS AN EMOTION some of us spend a lifetime dodging. Whether through distraction, drugs or even depression, we avoid unanesthetized pain. How strange it is, therefore, to hear Jesus encourage tears.

"Blessed are those who mourn," Jesus said, "for they will be comforted" (Matthew 5:4). We can't help but wonder what exactly we should mourn. With this beatitude immediately following the words, "Blessed are the poor in spirit," it's natural for us to think of mourning over our sins. Those who grieve all the ways they have displeased God will, like the prodigal son, be comforted by his gracious forgiveness and warm acceptance. Anyone who has come to the end of themselves, only to be enveloped by the relentless love of God, knows that sorrow over sin is a pathway to joy.

Or we might apply Christ's words to our mourning over the sins of others. Whether our heart is broken by the rebellion of a loved one or the universal waywardness of humanity, disregard for the ways of God can drive us to tears. We grieve what it has cost—and what it will cost—God's creation to thumb its nose at one so loving. Such sorrow yields intimacy with Jesus, a fellowship of suffering with the king who wept as he rode a donkey through a palm-branch gauntlet of shallow praise. To feel Christ's empathy as we mourn such wasted potential is strangely comforting.

But if the words of Jesus made Matthew think of the grief felt by those who hunger and thirst for righteousness, they must have made Luke long for the day when the godly will have the last laugh. "Blessed are you who weep now"—those were the words he was told Jesus used—"for you will laugh" (Luke 6:21). And then, a few breaths later, the converse: "Woe to you who laugh now, for you will mourn and weep" (Luke 6:25). Right now, in this upside-down world, it is the ungodly who are care-free and the godly whose hearts are heavy. But it is a temporary anomaly. In the Great Reversal that is coming, those who were persecuted for the sake of righteousness will be rewarded with sweet vindication, and those who thought they could enjoy sin and mistreat saints with impunity will find out how mistaken they were.

But might there be an even simpler truth in this beatitude? Might Jesus be encouraging us not to deflect emotional pain? Did not his own weeping at the tomb of Lazarus send the same message? Do not those who cry easily tell those of us who cannot remember the last time we wept to drop our defenses and let the tears flow, for they summon the Father of compassion and the God of all comfort, the one who is close to the brokenhearted and saves those who are crushed in spirit? And do we not observe that those who cry easily also tend to laugh easily, while stoics are as numb to joy as they are to grief? Henri Nouwen said, "If we try to avoid sorrow at all costs, we may never taste joy." But he was not the first to say it. Jesus was.

What should you be sad about, but aren't? Why are you holding back tears?

Meekness

Matthew 5:5

If you have eyes to see, you will find injustice everywhere. There is something dark in human nature that causes us to leverage our advantages over others. Dominance trumps decency. Might bullies right. Whether in war or wages, politics or peacekeeping, litigation or leadership, the goal is victory, not mercy. Love is sacrificed on the altar of power.

And just as it is the nature of the powerful to oppress, it is instinct of the oppressed to push back. When we are treated unfairly, we protest, resist, appeal, sue, organize, march, riot, overthrow—because we are as mad as hell and we're not going to take it anymore.

But amid all the punching and counterpunching, there are those who endure injustice quietly. Their passivity is often misdiagnosed as resignation. It is not resignation. It is patience.

"Blessed are the meek," Jesus said, "for they will inherit the earth" (Matthew 5:5). What is meekness? It is not weakness. It is the strength to let God fight for you, in his own time. And that time is not now. But the day will come when justice rolls down like a river, and the ones who will rule cities and nations will be those who waited on the Lord rather than taking matters into their own hands.

Jesus was not advocating a new response to injustice, but an old one. He was simply quoting Psalm 37:11, which is the climax of a passage that massages the knots out of the soul tensed up by tyranny.

Think of that situation in your life in which you are tempted to fight back.

Now, listen to the whisper of God's Spirit: "Do not fret because of those who are evil or be envious of those who do wrong; for like the grass they will soon wither, like green plants they will soon die away. Commit your way to the Lord; trust in him and he will do this: he will make your righteous reward shine like the dawn, your vindication like the noonday sun. Be still before the Lord and wait patiently for him; do not fret when people succeed in their ways, when they carry out their wicked schemes. Refrain from anger and turn from wrath; do not fret— it leads only to evil. For those who are evil will be destroyed, but those who hope in the Lord will inherit the land *(earth)*. A little while, and the wicked will be no more; though you look for them, they will not be found. But the meek will inherit the land *(earth)* and enjoy peace and prosperity" (Psalm 37:1-11).

That's not just what Jesus preached; it's also what he practiced. "I am meek and humble in heart," he said (Matthew 11:29). When others hurled their insults at him, he did not retaliate; when he suffered, he made no threats. Instead, he entrusted himself to him who judges justly (1 Peter 1:23). And what did God the Father do? He exalted Jesus to the highest place and gave him the name that is above every other name, that at the name of Jesus every knee will bow (Philippians 2:9-10).

Exalting the meek is God's way. It's slow justice, but we'll live longer in the right-side-up world than we will in this upside-down era. So be strong, take heart, and wait for the Lord, like Jesus did.

What injustices cause you to weep or pound your fist on the table? Can you—will you—drop to your knees and entrust yourself to him who judges justly?

Hunger

MATTHEW 5:6; LUKE 6:21, 25

JESUS SAID THAT WHEN WE SEEK FIRST the kingdom of God, everything we need—including our daily bread—will be given to us. But unforgettable images fertilize troubling questions. We have seen flies land on a sad little boy with a bloated stomach, pencil-thin limbs and empty eyes, and we wonder, *What about him? What about the millions like him, some of whom are surely kingdom-seeking Christians? Why does Christ's promise not seem to apply to them? And even if they are not Christians, does not the heart of their maker break for them? Could he not find a way to satisfy their hunger?*

Jesus does not answer questions like these. Instead, he enlists us to feed them, one at a time, as if they were Jesus himself (Matthew 25:40). And he assures us that the day will come when he will right all wrongs. His imminent, unstoppable, eternal reign will make us forget the tragic abnormalities and injustices that so many experience in this cruel world. "Blessed are you who hunger now," the Lord said to a crowd that surely must have included many who were malnourished, "for you will be satisfied" (Luke 6:21). These words make us think of what the apostle John heard as he gazed at the vision of heaven given to him by the Spirit of God. He saw an uncountable multitude wearing white robes and worshiping the Lamb on the throne, and he heard the voice of an angel. "These are those who have come out of the great tribulation," the angel said. "Never again will they hunger; never again will they thirst" (Revelation 7:14, 16). That promise should bring us to tears. Those who are hungry now will be well-fed forever. Come, Lord Jesus.

But there is more than one kind of hunger. There are those with empty stomachs, and there are those with unsatiated souls. Luke the doctor thought of the former, but Matthew the tax collector had a personal history, and perhaps an ongoing struggle, that led him to apply Jesus' words to the latter. "Blessed are those who hunger and thirst for righteousness," he heard Jesus say, "for they will be filled" (Matthew 5:6). Blessed are those who are sick and tired of the sin they battle in their flesh and the evil that poisons this world. Blessed are those who ache for the day when all that opposes God, within and without, will be extinct—because the day will come when righteousness reigns. On that day, and forever after that day, those whose bodies suffered hunger will be satisfied, and those whose souls suffered frustration will be filled.

Perhaps the apostle Peter was thinking of this beatitude when, after lamenting the rampant ungodliness he saw in the world, he wrote: "But in keeping with [God's] promise we are looking forward to a new heaven and a new earth, where righteousness dwells" (2 Peter 3:13). Do Peter's words resonate with you? Do you, or does at least some part of you, hunger for righteousness? Or have the delicacies of this world been your buffet? "Woe to you who are well fed now," Jesus warned, "for you will go hungry" (Luke 6:25). In the new age that is dawning, the signature entrée will be that which, today, is merely an appetizer: righteousness.

How, specifically, will you be different when a hunger for righteousness replaces your appetite for sin?

Mercy

Matthew 5:7

In a world as broken as ours, you don't have to go far to find someone in need of mercy. No farther than a mirror, actually. Thank God that he forgives all our sins and heals all our diseases, that he redeems our lives from the pit and crowns us with love and compassion (Psalm 103:3-4).

We are told that his empathetic, judgment-free, self-sacrificing love is unconditional, but that's not quite true. Jesus said that there is one condition—not a pre-requisite so much as a post-requisite: we must extend to others the same mercy God has extended to us. We must give others a hand, like the good Samaritan did for the man who had been mugged (Luke 10:37). And we must give others a break, like the king did for his servant who was in debt up to his eyeballs (Matthew 18:27).

And if we don't?

Well, imagine approaching God with an unmerciful heart. You know he sent his son to acquit adulteresses, cleanse lepers and drive out legions of demons, and you desperately need him to be as compassionate toward you as he was to them. But rather than finding a warm and welcoming Father, you encounter an intimidating, stone-faced Judge. As you pour out your woes to him and plead for mercy, his countenance does not soften. Instead, he dispassionately reminds you of those moments since his grace came flooding into your life that you had the opportunity to give the same to others. Remember that homeless man who asked, not for money, but for a meal? The friend who betrayed you and later begged for forgiveness? The aging parent who could not bring herself to ask for what you knew she needed? That between-jobs couple in your social circle that might have been able to keep their home if enough friends pitched in? The son who longed for his parents' love even though he knew they disapproved of his lifestyle? How could you who received such lavish love from God be so stingy in paying it forward? Now you are the one in need, and there he stands, arms folded, shaking his head. With the measure you used, it is now being measured to you.

There were times when Jesus warned his followers of scenarios like this, but in the Sermon on the Mount he dreamed of a better future for us. "Blessed are the merciful," he said with a smile, "for they will be shown mercy" (Matthew 5:7). Happy are those whose hearts have been so transformed by the love and grace of God that they cannot help but do for others what he has done for them. Not only will they discover that mercy has a boomerang effect in human relationships, with mercy begetting mercy and softening the hard edges of life; they will also find God to be more kind than they dared hope he would be. Rather than waking up in heaven to a court appointment, they will see their Father running toward them with arms extended, tears running down his cheeks, shouting for the welcome-home party to begin. This is the future Jesus envisions for us, and this is why he calls us to give others a hand, and to give them a break.

Who needs a helping hand today? Who needs for you to give them a break? Will you?

MATTHEW 5:8

"Blessed are the pure in heart, for they will see God" (Matthew 5:8). How could anyone hear anything Jesus said after that? Both purifying one's heart and seeing God seem beyond the realm of possibility, at least in this life.

External purity—clean hands, to use the psalmist's words—may be achievable with rigorous effort, but the heart is deceitful above all things and beyond cure (Jeremiah 17:9). If our purity must go that deep, down to that part of us that is capable of imagining what we are too ashamed to admit, what hope is there for us?

The sixth beatitude must have sparked such thoughts in the minds of those who heard the Sermon on the Mount. And if it did, it accomplished one purpose for which the Spirit of God put those radical words on the tongue of Jesus. It created a poverty of spirit, a mourning over sin, a hunger and thirst for righteousness that made the Gospel the best news a weary seeker of God could ever hear. If we but confess our impurities and embrace Christ's sacrifice, the blood of Jesus makes us as white as snow in the holy eyes of God! One day we who know the condition of our heart better than anyone except God himself will see his face, in all its glory, with no guilt or shame obscuring our view or filling us with terror! What relief this promise brings!

But must we wait until we die to see God? What if Jesus was telling us, not just how to see the Holy One someday, but how to see him today? What if heart-level purity can open the eyes of our spirit to the face of God while we still live and breathe? And what if that kind of intimacy makes all unholy pleasures bland, even repulsive, by comparison?

William Featherston was just a teenager when he wrote the words *My Jesus, I love thee, I know thou art mine; for thee all the follies of sin I resign.* We fear that the hard work of holiness will yield no immediate reward, just a void where the thrill of sin once made us feel alive, albeit fleetingly. But out of the mouth of a babe came the same promise that spilled from the lips of Jesus: God's presence is the only spring of living water in this world of broken cisterns. Do you want that unparalleled pleasure badly enough to clean up, not just your act, but your heart as well?

What sinful folly must you renounce to fully enjoy the blessedness of intimacy with God?

Peacemaking

MATTHEW 5:9

Ask 100 people to describe God in one word, and not one would use the word peacemaker. It's just not what he's famous for. Love, power, holiness, grace—they would all make the list. But when was the last time you heard God described as a peacemaker?

Yet when Jesus chose a single trait that marks us as children of God, it was a commitment to promoting peace. "Blessed are the peacemakers," he said, "for they will be called children of God" (Matthew 5:9). Diffusing conflict and fostering reconciliation—this is what God does. And this is what godly people do. They notice enmity. They feel it. And they act to end it.

When friends become enemies, a peacemaker braves the gap. Though he knows he is seizing a dog by the ears, he takes the risk, because he values what is at stake, even if the combatants don't, blinded as they are by bitterness.

When a church fractures, it is the voice of a peacemaker that cries out in the wilderness between warring factions, begging both to fight for unity rather than victory. As others pick sides, she champions only love, truth's most persuasive apologetic, and she weeps when her one church becomes two, knowing that everyone has lost, none more than the seeker-turned-skeptic whose flickering wick of curiosity has been snuffed out by a family feud.

When nations are at war, a peacemaker reminds presidents and prime ministers of ancient alliances, focuses their vision on common hopes, and proposes sane compromises. He reaches out with empathy to his friend on the right, then to his friend on the left, and then he pulls them together, refusing to let go until hatred melts, trust sprouts, and six hands form an audacious sphere of peace that blesses millions.

When a wayward soul strays so far from God that she is no longer aware of his existence, let alone his love, a peacemaker sees beyond her sister's calloused demeanor into her wounded heart and builds a bridge of friendship. Whether it takes a single conversation or an entire lifetime, she waits patiently for the mask to drop and the heart to open, and then she tells the story that beckons the prodigal home.

And what is the story she tells? It is of a brokenhearted father. His children have left home—all of them, save one. One by one they have ventured out on their own, and one by one they have lost their way. The father would pursue them, but he is homebound by holiness. And they are no longer fit to be called his children, soiled as they are by their sin. The one remaining son, the only faithful one, watches his father's sad eyes scan the horizon, day after day.

Finally, the son says, "I will bring them home."

"Do you know what it will cost you?" the father replies.

"Yes. I'll go."

The son leaves home to search for the runaways. Finding them, he assures them that their father's arms are open wide, aching to welcome them home. And the debt they owe? He will pay it. One by one they shed their shame and head for home, while he sets his face like flint toward the cross, where he does pay, with his life. With his blood.

Such is the resolve of a peacemaker: reconciliation, at any price. Blessed is the son of God, blessed is the daughter of God, who takes up so heavy a mantle.

In what gap is the Spirit of God asking you to stand, and at what price?

Persecution

Matthew 5:10-12

IF YOU THINK OF PERSECUTION IN RELATIVE TERMS, you may feel you have been dealt a fortunate hand. There are disciples of Jesus in other parts of the world whose allegiance and convictions are identical to yours but whose suffering is so severe you cannot bear to think about it. Limbless orphans and ravished widows, disfigured prisoners and headless martyrs—surely these are the brave saints Jesus was thinking of when he said, "Blessed are those who are persecuted because of righteousness, for theirs is the kingdom of heaven" (Matthew 5:10). *Amen*, we say. *This world is not worthy of them.* Their sacrifice silences us and their reward consoles us. To use the word persecution to describe our mild mistreatments feels dishonoring to those who have paid a much higher price for following Jesus.

Yet Jesus was not just thinking of them when he spoke of the blessings of persecution. He was also thinking of us. "Blessed are you when people insult you, persecute you and falsely say all kinds of evil against you because of me. Rejoice and be glad, because great is your reward in heaven"—and then he went so far as to include us in the company of those who, like so many of our brothers and sisters today, fertilized the seeds of truth with their own blood—"for in the same way they persecuted the prophets who were before you" (Matthew 5:11-12).

What an honor to be spoken of in the same breath as these heroes, merely because we have been insulted and slandered in Jesus' name.

But however small our sufferings seem by comparison, they wound us and weigh on us nonetheless. Jesus did not minimize the marginalization, the ridicule, the judgment, the disrespect, the exclusion we face in a society that, ironically, prides itself on its tolerance. For nothing more than modeling our lives after this man who is universally acknowledged as the embodiment of love, for merely agreeing with his bondage-breaking words of truth, for simply obeying him to whom all authority in heaven and on earth has been given, we are—yes—persecuted.

And for this Jesus tells us to rejoice, because whatever price we pay for loyalty to him on earth will be recompensed so disproportionately in heaven that we may wish we had suffered more. If death is the end, then we of all people are to be pitied, but if it is the beginning, we of all people are to be envied—for this dark strain of persecution is but the prelude to an endless symphony of joy.

In what insults, persecution or slander can you rejoice today because of the great reward that is waiting for you when God rights all wrongs?

LUKE 6:26

THERE IS A DIFFERENCE between reputation and character. Reputation is what others think of you. Character is who you really are. It is true that a person of good character tends to enjoy a good reputation, but when reputation becomes paramount, character may be sacrificed. "Woe to you when everyone speaks well of you," Jesus said, "for that is how their ancestors treated the false prophets" (Luke 6:26).

Perhaps one of those ancient prophets started well. He sought, not the deafening applause of people, but the quiet whisper of God. When he returned from the wilderness with clear and piercing words, the residue of the Spirit was palpable. The prophet came to be honored as a brave spokesman of truth, unfazed by the response of the people (approving though it always was).

Then came the day when the word of God clashed with the will of the majority. The prophet anticipated the inevitable friction, and it terrified him. His first words upon his return were trial balloons, spoken in hushed tones to loyal encouragers. Smiles melted into frowns, and soon he had nothing but suspicious critics, wondering if he had gotten too big for his britches. "Does God speak only to you?" they asked. Never before had his ability to hear from God been questioned. Never before had he questioned it himself. But now his reputation was at stake, his precious reputation, and the only thing to do was that which had always worked before—to say what made the people look up to him. So sharp edges were softened, disclaimers added, uncertainty expressed, dissenting opinions welcomed. His reputation was salvaged, but at what cost?

Jesus often withdrew to lonely places to pray. He always re-emerged saying exactly what the Father wanted him to say, exactly how he wanted him to say it. His reputation suffered irretrievably. Siblings said he lost his mind. Respected leaders labeled him a demon-possessed blasphemer. Even his closest friends rebuked him. Yet the word of God was like a fire shut up in his bones. He could not but speak.

Ultimately there was only one way to silence him, and that was to nail him to a cross.

The reputation of the man who died that day was in tatters, but never has anyone displayed such character.

Which do you want more—a good reputation or a blameless character? Decide carefully, because the day will come when you cannot have both.

In what way have you sacrificed character on the altar of reputation? How can you right this wrong?

Salt

Matthew 5:13

IT IS INEVITABLE that the resolve to follow Jesus will be threatened by the attractions and distractions of life in this world, and as our zeal cools the hope grows that God will still use us, half-hearted as we are.

But, though a bruised reed Jesus would never break, a lukewarm disciple he cannot stomach.

"You are the salt of the earth," he said to those who received his most challenging words with joy (Matthew 5:13). They were determined to live a counter-cultural life—a life of peace, purity, mercy and meekness despite poverty, grief, hunger and mistreatment. Indeed, to the extent that the beatitudes shape our lives, we season this bland planet with a tantalizing taste of otherworldliness.

Later Jesus would attribute saltiness to those who would rather gouge out an eye or lop off a limb than displease God or mislead a child (Mark 9:42-50). And those who renounce family, embrace suffering and liquidate assets, they are salty too (Luke 14:26-33).

The standards are stringent, yes, but if we want to be used by God, we must stand out, not blend in.

We have known this from the beginning, and yet, as sodium chloride melts away from minerals when it is immersed in water, leaving nothing but tasteless gravel, we lose everything that makes us useful to God when we re-acclimate to the world we left behind.

Honesty compels us to admit that we have lost our first love, but we lean hard on the grace of God, sincerely sorry for our backsliding, genuinely wishing we had done better, but strangely numb to revival. Surely God will still use us, though, impotent as we are. Right?

Wrong. "If the salt loses its saltiness, how can it be made salty again?" Jesus said. "It is no longer good for anything, except to be thrown out and trampled underfoot" (Matthew 5:13).

How harsh true love can be.

Am I irretrievably useless? we wonder—but the grief and fear with which we ask the question suggest that it's not too late to heed the words of the one whose distant voice we can scarcely make out: "Consider how far you have fallen! Repent and do the things you did at first" (Revelation 2:5).

What did you used to do that made you more salty than you are now? Why can't you do it again?

Light

MATTHEW 5:14-16

SECLUSION CAN MAKE even the most extraordinary people underestimate their potential impact on others, for how do we know we are anything other than ordinary unless we mingle?

Saying grace before meals. Humming hymns while doing chores. Avoiding exaggeration on timecards and expense reports. Noticing what weighs on the hearts of others. Filtering media options through the grid of godly values. Buying less in order to share more. Welcoming interruptions. Responding to news of tragedy with spontaneous prayer. These seem like common habits to you as a follower of Jesus, but do you know how abnormal they are to others in your community?

Perhaps not, if you live a sequestered life. Better to cluster with comrades than to be the oddball in more secular circles, right? It's less awkward for everyone.

But Jesus has not transformed us only to quarantine us. To the contrary, he said: "You are the light of the world. A town built on a hill cannot be hidden. Neither do people light a lamp and put it under a bowl. Instead they put it on its stand, and it gives light to everyone in the house" (Matthew 5:14-15). It is precisely because we are different—"salty", to use his word (Matthew 5:13)—that mere sociability makes us potent. For our lifestyle is as intriguing to others as it is unspectacular to us.

We do not know, sheltered as we are, how directionless, how turbulent, how hollow are the lives of those who seem to have everything except the one essential thing. But Jesus knows, and this is why he scatters us throughout the community like streetlights in subdivisions. And when we have the courage to take our lamp out from under the bowl and put it on its stand, behaving authentically and speaking without filters, stereotypes melt and curiosity grows.

"If even our left hand is not to know what our right hand is doing," we ask, "why should our neighbors know?" Because it's not about us; it's about a God in heaven who first sent Jesus and is now sending us to illuminate the world to his love. So "let your light shine before others, that they may see your good deeds and glorify your Father in heaven" (Matthew 5:16). In other words, get out more.

Where do you need to go, and what do you need to say, to let your light shine into the life of someone God has put on your heart?

Rules

Matthew 5:17

WE WANT TO PLEASE GOD, so we are given laws to obey and rules to follow. The laws came down from Mt. Sinai on stone tablets. The rules came down from the boardroom of whatever institution we have joined that purports to help us live a life of obedience. The intent of the rules is to ensure that we keep the laws. They are the pickets of the fence that keeps us a safe distance away from transgression. Keep the rules, the thinking goes, and you'll never break the law.

But if the rules eclipse the law, so much so that what is written in stone is forgotten, and righteousness is gauged by rule-keeping at the expense of law-keeping, our perspective might become so perverted that we will condemn an innocent man. Why, we might even misjudge the Messiah.

Jesus socialized with those who had a checkered past, and the Pharisees snorted, "Why do you eat and drink with tax collectors and sinners?" (Luke 5:30). Of course we should love our neighbors, but at the risk of contamination? Never.

Jesus told a man who hadn't been on his feet for 38 years to pick up his mat and walk, and the religious leaders put out an APB on Jesus for inciting the man to bear the load of his mat on the Sabbath day, something that was clearly against the rules (John 5:8-10).

Jesus un-shriveled a man's hand in church, and to the guardians of the rules, it was a capital offense (Mark 3:6). The Sabbath was far too holy a day to do the work of healing; weren't six days a week enough for that?

On another Sabbath, Jesus gave sight to a man who had been blind since birth, and the Pharisees repeated their gnat-straining, camel-swallowing chorus: "This man is not from God, for he does not keep the Sabbath" (John 9:16).

Jesus refused to rebuke his followers for eating with unwashed hands, and his opponents wondered aloud why he didn't teach them to "live in accordance with the tradition of the elders" (Mark 7:5). He responded with a question of his own: "And why do you break the command of God for the sake of your tradition?" (Matthew 15:3) Then he gave an example: the Corban rule, by which they dedicated their material possessions to God in order to dodge their responsibility to care for their fathers and mothers. Christ's disciples tried to talk him down, but instead he gassed the fire by calling the Pharisees blind guides who were unworthy of being followed into the pit.

How ironic that the one whose finger etched the commandments into stone was accused of playing fast and loose with the law. He broke so many rules that he was branded a rebel. A heretic. A demon. Follow him at your own risk, the leaders said.

But Jesus said, "Do not think that I have come to abolish the Law or the Prophets; I have not come to abolish them but to fulfill them" (Matthew 5:17). His issue was not with the laws; it was with the rules. And if we learn nothing else from his example, we can hardly miss this: sometimes, in order to obey the law, you have to break the rules.

Are you more likely to break the rules in order to obey God's law, or to break his law in order to keep the rules? What does your track record reveal?

Law

Matthew 5:18

LIKE AN OCEAN BREEZE blowing through a petrified forest, the ministry of Jesus aerated the ancient, unyielding harshness of the Law with the refreshing simplicity of love. So all-encompassing was his ethic and so compelling was his practice of it that the Law seemed like a relic, supplanted by the personification of a better way. No one missed the stodgy old rule book, save those whose power derived from their adherence to it.

How strange, therefore, that when he spoke of the Law, Jesus sided with the traditionalists. It sounded almost like a contradiction to his own revolutionary lifestyle for him to say, "Truly I tell you, until heaven and earth disappear, not the smallest letter, not the least stroke of a pen, will be any means disappear from the Law until everything is accomplished" (Matthew 5:18). How could Jesus say anything positive about a legal code that had proven incapable of producing a God-pleasing life? Why would he endorse that which his own behavior rendered obsolete?

How forgetful of us to ask such questions. Was it really that long ago that we were smug with self-righteousness, thinking so highly of ourselves that we felt no need for a Savior? Whatever the reasons for Christ's crucifixion, it never occurred to us that we might be to blame—until that pang of guilt we felt when we heard, "Thou shalt not commit adultery," as if for the first time. "Honor thy father and mother" suddenly morphed from a slogan to an indictment. "Thou shalt not take the name of the Lord thy God in vain" was no longer a verse we learned in Sunday school, but a whisper we heard after a profanity-laced tirade. Why, we couldn't even fill out a tax form without the words "Thou shalt not steal" haunting our conscience. Whether slowly or suddenly, it dawned on us—thanks to the Law—that we were sinners. And it was only then that the formerly irrelevant death of Jesus became the most precious gift ever given. To have that ever-accusing written code nailed to the cross of Christ—oh, what liberation!

And now we who are acutely aware of our sinfulness pray for those who are oblivious to theirs. We love them deeply and want them to feel the forgiveness we have felt and to share the hope we have. But why would they need Jesus? They are good people, after all, at least when they compare themselves to others. If hell is for anybody, it's certainly not for them. But perhaps, as he whispered to us, the Spirit will whisper to them the condemning words of God's Law, which, while lacking the power to make them righteous, might just give them eyes to see themselves as they really are. Then, and only then, will they see Jesus as he really is.

This is the longing of our hearts, and to an infinitely greater degree, the heart of Jesus. It is because of his passionate, pulsating love for those we most want to be with us in heaven that, until heaven and earth disappear, not the smallest letter, not the least stroke of a pen, will be any means disappear from the Law. Only when it leads every last chosen one into the merciful arms of Jesus will its purpose be accomplished.

Who, among those you love, needs God's Law to lead them to God's Son? How can your prayers help?

Greatness

Matthew 5:19

What Jesus said about the Law of God would have settled the nerves of those who doubted his orthodoxy if only his practice matched his preaching.

"Anyone who sets aside one of the least of these commands and teaches others accordingly will be called least in the kingdom of heaven," he said, "but whoever practices and teaches these commands will be called great in the kingdom of heaven" (Matthew 5:19). The commands he was referring to were those in God's Law—his perfect, trustworthy, precious Law. You can almost hear the "Amens" of the clergymen in the crowd.

But no sooner did Jesus exalt the Law than he started editing it. Anger became as felonious as murder. Adultery became a sin of the mind as well as the body. Divorce became taboo, certificate or not. No longer was anything that went into the body unclean, just that which came out of the heart. Rest on the Sabbath became unholy if it trumped love. Every command and prohibition inscribed in stone was reduced to a simple maxim: Do to others what you would have them do to you. There's no denying the fact that, when it came to the letter of the Law, Jesus set aside some of the least of God's commands and taught others to do the same.

What a curious way to be confronted with the question, "Who do you say I am?" There are only two kinds of people who would dare to treat God's Law as a living document: a hell-bound heretic, or God himself.

How much easier it would have been if the miracles of Jesus were paired with teaching that was always undeniably orthodox. A Messiah who did the impossible and parroted the Torah—who wouldn't follow such a man? Instead, we must decide what to do with this wonder-working Law-tweaker. Is he to be called least in the kingdom of heaven, or worse, a son of hell? Or is he to be worshiped as Lord and God?

Those of us who have gone all-in on the deity of Jesus no longer have the luxury of interpreting God's Law on our own. Instead, we filter it through the inerrant commentary of the unconventional Christ. Great in the kingdom of heaven are those who practice and teach his commands, for to do so is to fulfill the Law of God.

What Old Testament law has taken on new significance for you because of how Jesus re-framed it?

MATTHEW 5:20

IT IS IRONIC that so much acrimony existed between Jesus and the Pharisees, considering how much they had in common. Their shared reverence for God's Law was unparalleled, and so too was their agreement that righteousness required more than mere adherence to what was written on tablets of stone.

It was what they added that took them on divergent paths. The Pharisees added breadth; Jesus, depth. Their quest was for comprehensiveness; his, for distillation. There was no end to the rules they added to God's original 613, for without specific instructions for every contingency of life, how could anyone be sure they were pleasing God? Jesus, in contrast, excavated from the laws underlying principles that, at sufficient depth, revealed a common origin. Who would have thought that a single maxim could guide all of life?

So when Jesus said, "I tell you that unless your righteousness surpasses that of the Pharisees and the teachers of the law, you will certainly not enter the kingdom of heaven" (Matthew 5:20), he was not questioning their zeal but rejecting their approach. In their obsession to keep the rules, they missed the point.

To say that their legalism had become ludicrous may be mystifying in the abstract, but one needs only to log time in the

Talmud (the authorized Jewish commentary on God's law) to find endless concrete examples of nit-picky regulations designed to apply extraordinary creativity to the avoidance of breaking laws while doing whatever one wants to do. What kind of God did they think they could impress by jumping through so many loopholes? But to list examples feels cruel, as if doing so would expose a friend's most shameful secrets.

Yet, astoundingly, they were not embarrassed by their legal code; they were proud of it. In fact, they peddled it as the way of righteousness, putting others under the same load they had grown accustomed to bearing. This was what Jesus could not stomach. To deceive oneself is tragic; but to proselytize others into an exhausting way of life that leads only to alienation from God is unconscionable. Jesus had to call them out, lest those who had lost their way under Pharisaic influence be forever wandering in the wilderness.

But the alternative Jesus proposed, though far simpler, was no less daunting. What is at the core of God's laws? Is it not love? Does not every law emanate from that singular ethic? So, then, can I say I am not a murderer only because I do not pull the trigger of a gun that is aimed at someone I am furious with? Are words not bullets?

Am I acquitted from the charge of adultery merely because I do not act out the fantasy that plays in my brain? Does not love prohibit me from even thinking about what I have the self-control not to do?

Is divorce any less devastating simply because I do it by the book? Is not a vow broken before its expiration date an inexcusable betrayal?

In terms of weight, Jesus offered rest for the weary, a lighter burden than the legal library of the Pharisees, but how easy is the yoke of love? If we can pull off obedience to the letter of the Law but violate its intent, can we honestly claim that our righteousness surpasses that of the Pharisees? Or are we, like them, desperately in need of a clean slate and a new heart?

Which of God's laws are you fulfilling to the letter but violating in spirit?

Anger

MATTHEW 5:21-22

"I HAVE NEVER MURDERED ANYONE." Among those who are convinced they do not deserve to go to hell, no defense is more common.

But to think that a homicide-free past guarantees a heavenly future reveals an alarming ignorance about God's standards. Jesus said: "You have heard that it was said to the people long ago, 'You shall not murder, and anyone who murders will be subject to judgment.' But I tell you that anyone who is angry with a brother or sister will be subject to judgment. Again, anyone who says to a brother or sister, 'Raca,' is answerable to the court. And anyone who says, 'You fool!' will be in danger of the fire of hell" (Matthew 5:21-22).

Oh, my. How do we elude such damning words? With yes-but questions. *Yes, but who are my brothers and sisters?* Even if Jesus was referring specifically to others in the community of faith, excusing our anger toward those outside that circle makes us as guilty of the very nit-picking Jesus condemns.

Yes, but what about righteous anger? To point out that Jesus himself was livid on occasion—toward greedy merchants in the temple and heartless snobs in the synagogue—or that he sometimes called both Pharisees and disciples fools is of course true, but when has our anger been so purely righteous? Honesty compels us to admit that we marinate in the very poison that motivates those with less self-control to kill. Woe to us.

But these were not words spoken merely to reduce us to poverty of spirit, though that is a good start. No, they were also intended to intensify our hunger for righteousness. True, we have an anger problem. Now, what are we going to do about it? What fruit will our repentance bear?

Perhaps the fruit of self-examination. *What does my rage toward him, toward her, toward them, say about me? Search me, O God, and know my heart. See if there be any wicked way in me.*

And graciousness. *O Lord, make me slow to anger, and quick to forgive, as you are. Do not let the sun go down on my anger. Excise it from my heart before bitterness takes root.*

And restraint. *I know that words kill, Spirit of God, so do not let any unwholesome talk come out of my mouth—not "Raca", not "You fool"—but only what is helpful for building others up according to their needs, that it may benefit those who listen.*

This world is a cauldron that bubbles with animosity, grudges, slander and, yes, murder. Age does not mellow us; it brings long-accumulated anger close to the surface, ever poised to vent—unless the stubborn, unrelenting Spirit of God draws the venom out of our heart. Blessed are those who submit to such excruciating sanctification. And blessed are all whose offenses are overlooked by one so Christlike.

With whom are you so angry that forgiveness is possible only with the help of the Holy Spirit?

Reconciliation

MATTHEW 5:23-24

YOU LONG TO WORSHIP GOD with the concentration he deserves, but your mind is a tree full of monkeys. Unfinished tasks, unpaid bills, unanswered questions, unfulfilled dreams, unconquerable fears—they gibber and jump across synapses, making stillness elusive. Yet you are determined, on this holy day, to quell distractions and offer to God an undivided heart, singular in its focus and undiluted in its reverence. He is worthy of no less.

And you are almost there, almost euphoric in worship, nearly intoxicated with the love of God, when the face of a brother or the silhouette of a sister interrupts your intimacy with the Holy One. How dare they trespass this sacred moment! Hasn't their resentment stolen enough joy from you already? To be so prickly, so easily provoked, by such a minor offense. To hold such a stubborn grudge. Why, others have done far worse to you countless times, and you were quick to forgive, giving them the same grace that you have been given. But this bitter brother, this outraged sister, couldn't let it go. They magnified what should have been minimized. Ultimately you decided they were unappeasable, and you moved on. It's their problem, not yours.

But now here they are, standing between you and God, arms crossed. Finally, you concede, *I really should try again to make amends. And I will. But not right now. Not during this precious time of worship.*

Now there is another figure in your mind's eye. Jesus. Standing next to the offended one, further obscuring your vision of the Almighty. The volume of the music fades, and you hear his inaudible, familiar voice: "If you are offering your gift at the altar and there remember that your brother or sister has something against you, leave your gift there in front of the altar. First go and be reconciled to them; then come and offer your gift" (Matthew 5:23-24).

Now?

Now.

A silent argument ensues, but your protests are no match for the conviction of the Holy Spirit. Finally, in grim obedience, you gather your belongings and scooch past others, disrupting their Godward focus. You tiptoe up the dimly lit aisle, head down, feeling the judgment of a hundred pairs of eyes. Now you are squinting in the sunshine, sleepwalking toward your car, turning left instead of right out of the parking lot, because you are not going to your home but to theirs, and you know the way because you drove it a thousand times before that day when everything changed. The car seems to be on autopilot. Your mind is elsewhere. Every word you rehearse sounds lame. You feel like a fool, taking Jesus so literally.

And then you are there. Your legs ignore the objections of your heart and march your body toward certain disaster. You watch your arm reach out, you see your fist tighten, you hear the three faint knocks of your knuckles on the door. You pray they are not home.

But, alas, the door opens—and there they are. It is the first time your eyes have met since that terrible day, and suddenly you realize that no words are necessary. They know why you are there, and tears begin to flow—first down their face, now down yours. You are in each other's arms, tears smearing tears, repentance and forgiveness co-mingling. What haunted you for years is gone in a moment. You have your friend back, and the gratitude you feel ascends to the nostrils of God as a sweet-smelling aroma, the most beautiful worship he has received from you in a very long time.

With whom do you need to be reconciled between now and the next time you offer your gift at the altar of God?

Grudges

MATTHEW 5:25-26

TODAY YOU ARE ONE DAY CLOSER to the Day of Judgment than you were yesterday—you, and the one who has hurt you so deeply. Though you do not walk together as you once did, there is still a sense in which you are side-by-side, for you will arrive at the courthouse of the Lord on the same day. It is a day you look forward to, truth be told, because you know the wrong that has been done to you will finally be made right.

Jesus' words of warning to your betrayer are music to your ears. "Settle matters quickly with your adversary who is taking you to court. Do it while you are still together on the way, or your adversary may hand you over to the judge, and the judge may hand you over to the officer, and you may be thrown into prison. Truly I tell you, you will not get out until you have paid the last penny" (Matthew 5:25-26). Ah, justice at last!

What has never occurred to you, not once, is that you might be the guilty party.

After all, you were the victim, not the perpetrator. You have every right to be angry. Who would not take offense at such malice? Anyone in your shoes would look forward to seeing the tables turned.

And yet Jesus said, with no disclaimers, that anger will incur judgment, as surely as murder will. How ironic that the one who has wounded you is the very one who is pressing charges against you for the grudge you nurse toward them! And if nothing changes, if you do not forgive your brother or sister before your court date, a prison sentence is inevitable. Yes, for you, one whose name has been indelibly recorded in the Lamb's book of life.

You cannot help but wonder, *How could I—a heaven-bound, forgiven, justified saint, one whose scarlet sins have been made whiter than snow by the blood of Christ—be ordered by my Father-Judge to do prison time? And for something done to me, not by me?* It simply does not compute. There must be some mistake.

While you are trying to solve this eschatological riddle, make room for this question: Are you presently free? Since the day your former friend scarred you, have you experienced the liberation you felt when you first fell in love with Jesus? Do you still see the beauty of the world in high saturation hues, or has it become faded and colorless? Is joy as joyful and sorrow as sorrowful, or is your heart growing ever more numb? Is each morning bright with promise, or a rerun of yesterday's tedium? Do you feel as if life is an adventure, or a prison sentence?

What if you have already had your day in court? What if, though you could not hear the voice of God, deafened as you were by bitterness, he said to you, "You wicked servant! I canceled all that debt of yours because you begged me to. Shouldn't you have had mercy on your fellow servant just as I had on you?" (Matthew 18:32-33). And what if, in his anger, your master locked you in a prison of your own making, to be tortured until you pay back all you owe—or until you forgive your brother or sister from the heart?

Or what if, by God's mercy, today you find yourself in the fleeting interval between offense and imprisonment? Better to settle matters quickly than to acidify slowly.

What do you have to lose by forgiving the one who has hurt you most deeply? What do you have to gain?

Adultery

Matthew 5:27-28

Sometimes we see God's Law in black and white so that we can loiter in gray. As long as we don't cross his line in the sand, we can trespass the less conspicuous boundaries of our conscience with impunity.

Adultery, according to the letter of the Law, occurs when a man has sex with a woman who is married or engaged to another man. How many impure thoughts could one have, how many unholy actions could one take, how many habits could one form, without breaking God's law?

Jesus did more than broaden adultery to include any and every violation of marriage vows. He also deepened it, defining it as a sin that could be committed not just with the body, but also with the mind: "You have heard that it was said, 'You shall not commit adultery.' But I tell you that anyone who looks at a woman lustfully has already committed adultery with her in his heart" (Matthew 5:27-28). He was not talking about a look that mutates into lust, but a look that is motivated by lust. We may insist that our lust is accidental, but Jesus said it is intentional. The blame belongs, not to the desirability of the person who is being looked at, but to the depravity of the person doing the looking.

Do we really grasp the implications of this paradigm shift? In Jewish law, adultery was punishable by death. Worse, the apostle Paul said that adulterers will not inherit the kingdom of God. Ponder this: the wages of lust is hell. There but for the grace of God go all of us.

The more intensely we feel the white-hot holiness of God, the more astounded we are by the story of the woman caught in adultery by a posse of adulterers. Which is more mind-boggling—the mercy of Jesus, or the obliviousness of the accusers? They were eager to stone the adulteress to death, but were they prepared to be judged by God with the same measure that they were using to condemn her? When Jesus said, "Let any of you who is without sin be the first to throw a stone at her" (John 8:7), he was not just protecting her; he was also protecting them.

Dropping the rocks we are tempted to hurl at others is insufficient. The words of Jesus expose the filth in our own souls, and if they don't elicit confession and repentance and pleas for forgiveness, we know neither God nor ourselves.

Are you guilty of adultery? If so, what do you deserve? And what do you want to say to the God who does not treat you as your sins deserve?

Excision

Matthew 5:29-30

IF YOU WANT TO ELIMINATE LUST, you're going to have to do more than enucleate an eyeball or amputate a hand. Yes, Jesus said, "If your right eye causes you to stumble, gouge it out and throw it away. It is better for you to lose one part of your body than for your whole body to be thrown into hell. And if your right hand causes you to stumble, cut it off and throw it away. It is better for you to lose one part of your body than for your whole body to go into hell" (Matthew 5:29-30). But he did not say that lust's origin is in the eye or the hand. He said it is in the heart. So once you start cutting, where do you stop? And since no physical mutilation can slay the beast within, what hope do we have of avoiding hell? If these words of Jesus do not reduce us to utter poverty of spirit, the kingdom of heaven will never be ours.

Blessed are those who acknowledge that sin is a cancer of the heart that has metastasized to every cell in their body, for they are the ones with whom God has made a new covenant, mediated by Christ: "I will forgive their wickedness and will remember their sins no more" (Jeremiah 31:34). Nothing but the blood of Jesus can wash away the sin that our wicked heart pumps into our eyes, our hands, our every organ.

But there is more to the new covenant than forgiveness. "I will write my law on their hearts," declared the Lord (Jeremiah 31:33). And when our heart becomes the tablet upon which God writes his law, when it becomes the dwelling of his Spirit, we can no longer lust comfortably, shrugging our shoulders and claiming that the fight for purity is futile. Instead, we are compelled to gouge out and cut off whatever our flesh finds useful in its mutiny. Isolation. Images. Texts. Travel routes. Fantasies. Friendships. Remotes. Rendezvous. Phone numbers. Flirtation. Subscriptions. Substances.

No longer is the goal to avoid hell. It is to love God with all our heart, soul, mind and strength. It is to love our neighbor as ourselves. It is to become in real life what we already are in God's eyes, despite the unrelenting onslaught of evil from without and within.

And so, in view of God's mercy, which is new every morning and with every confession of sin, we offer our bodies as living sacrifices to him, and we offer the parts of our bodies to him as instruments of righteousness. Our eyes. Our hands. Our feet. Our ears. Our tongues. Our genitals. Our minds. Our hearts. In Jesus' name we forbid all those once hell-bound body parts to do the bidding of our flesh. Instead, we ready them to respond to the impulses of the Spirit, as did the body parts of Jesus himself, purifying this world with love, one look and one touch at a time.

What must be excised from your life in order for you to live in love instead of lust? What is preventing you from performing the amputation?

MATTHEW 5:31-32

IT HAS BEEN HANDLED BY SO MANY DIRTY HANDS, chipped and scratched by so many careless fumbles, coated by the tarnish of so much time, that it's hard to imagine the beauty of sex at the dawn of creation. Pure souls in perfect bodies, intimate with God and fully awake to the delicacies of the Garden, yet strangely incomplete. In each other the man and woman found companionship, but still there was distance, a longing to solve the mystery of this one so familiar and yet so different, so delightfully different. The desire, the need, to know and be known radiated from deep within and grew ever more intense as it reached the nerves below the skin. Touch multiplied the pleasure until it bordered on pain, and in the discovery of one another's body they were led to the most sensitive point of contact. It was not a rational decision, but a mutual, insatiable ache that brought them together, his body seeking permission to enter, hers giving it. At last the two were one—one flesh, one soul—communicating not with words but with touch, unrestrained and euphoric—and with their creator rejoicing. "Eat, O friends, and drink; drink your fill, O lovers!"

It was an act so intimate, so vulnerable, so bonding, that to ever trespass the boundaries of lifelong marriage, to sever soul and body and let one's springs overflow into the streets, would create a wound so deep it might never heal. A wound in the one for whom you vowed to forsake all others, yes, but also a wound in you. The seventh commandment—the prohibition of adultery—was never intended to limit pleasure, only to protect it from dilution, from pollution.

The world has unraveled so irretrievably that most are unable to appreciate the fragile glory of sex as God designed it. What was intended to be the most exquisite expression of faithful love has been reduced to hollow sensuality. How many today grasp that sex creates, not just symbolic oneness, but a real and irreversible amalgamation of souls? Can divorce papers put asunder what God has joined together? Can two people who once shared their bodies with one another make a clean, bloodless break and simply start over? Is divorce not rather the gruesome tearing apart of a single body?

Jesus was not ice-hearted toward those who could not undo the damage that divorce had done, but neither could he tame his passion to protect God's good gift. Thus he restrained his impulse to comfort, and instead he mended the fence his Father had placed around sex. "It has been said, 'Anyone who divorces his wife must give her a certificate of divorce.' But I tell you that anyone who divorces his wife, except for sexual immorality, makes her the victim of adultery, and anyone who marries a divorced woman commits adultery" (Matthew 5:31-32).

If there is any mercy in the premature death of a marriage, it is that it exposes our sinfulness, our brokenness, undeniably. And it is when we admit what is obvious that the grace of God bleaches our past, salves our wounds, and secures our inclusion in a new Garden of delights, where the former things—divorce included—are forgotten forever.

What sin have you committed that Jesus will not let you hide? Why do you think he wants you to admit the obvious?

Swearing

MATTHEW 5:33-37

OLD TESTAMENT PASSAGES about vows and oaths were the strips of duct tape with which God held together a society unriveted by dishonesty.

A simple prohibition should have been enough. "Do not lie" (Leviticus 19:11). But, with such rampant deceit, the people could not trust each other without the insurance of a sacred promise. Graciously, God accommodated their weakness by permitting vows and oaths. He even swore himself, not because it made his word more reliable, but because the depraved people did not expect anyone, not even God, to tell the truth without added incentive to do so.

Of course, honesty boosters could not reform them. They needed loopholes for their many infractions. And so they subdivided oaths and vows into those that were binding and those that were not. An entire volume of rabbinical hair-splitting was devoted to the subject. It was not swearing by the temple that required truthfulness, just swearing by the gold in the temple. And to swear by the altar was not binding, only to swear by the gift on the altar. One could even swear by heaven with impunity, as long as the God of heaven was not mentioned. And if a vow was made rashly, there was a ritual one could perform to annul it.

It was a convoluted code of legalism, but deft navigation of it was easier than honesty, and, in their minds, equally acquitting.

How perverted, we say—we who cross our heart in hope to die with fingers crossed, we who distinguish between bold-faced lies and little white lies, we who under threat of perjury must place our hand on a Bible and swear to tell the truth, the whole truth and nothing but the truth, so help us God.

There is no nation on earth, and no generation since the dawn of humanity, in which Jesus could have immersed himself without being consumed by a zeal for truthfulness. As the very image of the invisible God, his face could not but redden at such duplicity and such delusion. Idealistic as he must have sounded, his voice could not but express his vision of integrity restored. "You have heard that it was said to the people long ago, 'Do not break your oath, but fulfill to the Lord the vows you have made.' But I tell you"—and then came words that pierced through layers of technicalities and fumigated the hearts of those hungry for righteousness—"do not swear an oath at all: either by heaven, for it is God's throne; or by the earth, for it is his footstool; or by Jerusalem, for it is the city of the Great King. And do not swear by your head, for you cannot make even one hair white or black. All you need to say is simply 'Yes' or 'No'; anything beyond this comes from the evil one" (Matthew 5:33-37).

Yes. No. These are complete sentences in the kingdom of God.

In what area of your life have you rationalized dishonesty despite the convicting nudge of the Holy Spirit?

Self-Defense

MATTHEW 5:38-39

IT IS FAR EASIER TO DEBATE the societal ramifications of the Sermon on the Mount than it is to wrestle with its personal implications.

"You have heard that it was said, 'Eye for eye, and tooth for tooth' (Matthew 5:38). But I tell you...'"—and before he tells us, we find ourselves arguing either for or against retributive justice in the legal system—because, after all, wasn't that the issue in the passage (actually, passages—Exodus 21:23, Leviticus 24:20, and Deuteronomy 19:21) that he quoted? And it wasn't just eye for eye and tooth for tooth, but also life for life. We didn't invent the death penalty; God did. And so the question becomes, *Was Jesus for or against capital punishment?*

What a convenient dodge.

Remarkably, Jesus did not apply God's law to public policy, just to personal behavior. "But I tell you, do not resist an evil person. If anyone slaps you on the right cheek, turn to them the other cheek also" (Matthew 5:39). Whatever the appropriate legal punishment for an unprovoked attack, our personal response must not be revenge, or even escape. No, Jesus said we are to invite a repeat offense.

Does it not take your breath away to think of what it would be like to actually live this way? Imagine standing face-to-face with someone who is threatening physical harm because they are enraged by your convicting righteousness. Courageously, you refuse to be deterred. Suddenly their hand blurs upward, stunning you with a painful slap on the cheek. Every instinct tells you to turn and run. But in your spirit the words of Jesus echo: "Turn the other cheek." Your feet are anchors, but your neck pivots. Now your other cheek is defenselessly exposed.

No. Surely Jesus did not mean for us to take him literally! He must have been speaking metaphorically, using the physical blow to represent a verbal insult. He would not disparage self-defense, we insist.

But what do we make of the other times the Bible speaks of the kind of slap Jesus taught us to absorb? It occurs in three scenes, all in the hours between Christ's midnight arrest and his mid-morning execution.

After he was apprehended, Jesus was taken to the home of the high priest emeritus, Annas. His answer to one of Annas' questions offended an official, who proceeded to slap him in the face. "Kiss the Son, lest he be angry and you be destroyed in your way," Psalm 2:12 (NIV84) warns, "for his wrath can flare up in a moment." But rather than wrath, the official received a gentle answer from the immovable Son of God. "If I spoke the truth, why did you strike me?" (John 18:23).

Then Jesus was interrogated by Israel's religious leaders. Several witnesses swore to contradictory lies about him, but he did not speak in his own defense. He opened his mouth only once, to confirm that he was indeed the Messiah and the Son of God. Immediately cries of blasphemy detonated around the room, and the voice vote was unanimous: he must die. Whatever Jesus thought about the death penalty, the Sanhedrin believed in it—even for one who never injured so much as an eye or a tooth. Those guarding Jesus began punching him and spitting on him, and then they played a game. They blindfolded him, then slapped him in the face and said, "Prophesy to us, Messiah! Who hit you?" (Matthew 26:67-68). He did not speak. He did not resist. He simply turned to them the other cheek, which they proceeded to slap as well.

Finally, when the Roman governor washed his hands of guilt and surrendered Jesus to the frenzied mob, the soldiers flogged him, stripped him naked, robed him in scarlet, shoved a thorny crown on his head, put a staff in hand, knelt down and mockingly hailed him as King of the Jews, beat him over the head with the staff, spit on him, and—yes—slapped him in the face. He offered his cheeks to them, first one and then the other.

How literally must we be prepared to take Matthew 5:39? See the swollen, contused cheeks of your Lord, and you will have your answer.

In what ways are you being tempted to flee from, or retaliate against, mistreatment? What would "turning the other cheek" look like?

Litigation

MATTHEW 5:40

THERE ARE THOSE SO GREEDY AND STONE-HEARTED that, if they could, they would rob you of everything you own—if not under the cover of darkness, then under the legitimization of the court. A lawsuit may achieve justice, but too often it is sanctioned burglary. When you are sued unfairly, should you give the plaintiff everything they are demanding?

No. More.

"If anyone wants to sue you and take your shirt, hand over your coat as well," Jesus said (Matthew 5:40). His words sound tame to those of us with walk-in closets, but what if you owned nothing more than the clothes on your back? In Jesus' day, there were some so poor that, when they had to borrow money to survive, all they had to offer as collateral was their cloak—and it was against the law for the lender to keep it overnight, because it doubled as a blanket. Imagine being so destitute. How do the words of Jesus sound to you now? "If someone wants to sue you for half of all you own, give to them the other half as well."

It is such a radical saying that it must be hyperbole. Surely Jesus is merely prodding us to be generous even to the malicious. But if we are actually sued unjustly, it's time to lawyer up, right?

The apostle Paul addressed this very question in 1 Corinthians 6. When he rebuked the Christians in Corinth for suing one another in civil court, thus violating the unity that makes Jesus unignorable to the world, they must have breathed a sigh of relief and begun their search for Christian arbitrators. But then Paul said: "The very fact that you have lawsuits among you means you have been completely defeated already. Why not rather be wronged? Why not rather be cheated?" (1 Corinthians 6:7).

This is the spirit of what Jesus taught. And if the willingness to give your adversary more than they are demanding from you applies in the courtroom, it applies as well in the conference room, in the classroom, in the family room—indeed in any room where you feel you are being cheated.

If this is a bar too high for you to clear, if you must admit that you would never give to someone more than they are demanding from you, then you are not far from the kingdom of God that belongs to the poor in spirit. Mourn the fact that you are not perfect, as your heavenly Father is perfect, and hunger and thirst for a righteousness so Christlike that you would give all you possess to your enemy.

Who is demanding from you more than they have a right to ask? How can you exceed their expectations?

Kindness

Matthew 5:41

Dignity is in our DNA. We know, instinctively, that as human beings we bear the image of God, that he has made us a little lower than the angels and crowned us with glory and honor. It is not sinful pride that makes us hold our head high; it is a sense of worth that those who are so obviously God's workmanship cannot help but feel.

So to have our dignity trodden underfoot by a fellow human being—to be treated as if we are of less value than them, whether because of race, gender or rank, is deeply insulting. How dare they look down their nose at us? We would never stand for it if not for the fact that, in this broken world of ours, power is distributed unequally, and it is the better part of wisdom not to push back against those who lord it over us.

So many times in history the Jewish race has been treated ignobly. In Jesus' day, a Roman soldier could, on a whim, unload whatever he was carrying onto the nearest Jew. By law, the Israeli citizen was compelled to take 1,000 steps, a mile's worth, with the soldier's load on his or her own back.

Imagine the inconvenience, the humiliation, the resentment. It is not hard for you to do if you have been the victim of authority abuse. Who has leveraged power at your expense? A supervisor? A police officer? A parent? No doubt it has taken extraordinary restraint for you to silently comply.

If Jesus were to address only your attitude, if he were to tell you to endure such unjust mistreatment with no thought of revenge, only graciousness, that would be challenge enough. But he advocates an even more audacious response: "If anyone forces you to go one mile, go with them two miles" (Matthew 5:41). Whatever is demanded of you, do double that.

Think of how contrary such advice is to a demand for justice. Do you have a right to object? To file a complaint? To march in protest? Of course. But pushing back has never changed a human heart. Resistance only intensifies the determination to dominate, perpetuating subjugation. Do you want to heap burning coals of shame on a bully's head? Do twice what they demand. Even if such costly obedience never softens the heart of the oppressor, it warms the heart of God. Blessed are those whose response to injustice is patterned after Jesus, who not only forgave his killers, but went the second mile by transferring to them his righteousness so that they, of all people, could be perfect in the eyes of God.

At whose hands are you suffering indignity or injustice right now? What is a practical way to give them twice what they are demanding from you?

Generosity

MATTHEW 5:42

A MAN WHO LIVED JUST ACROSS THE BORDER from Tijuana, Mexico wanted to plant a church among the poor who lived in the slums outside the city. Circumstances prevented him from moving to Mexico, so he drove south through the border bottleneck three days a week in a pick-up truck, returning home late at night through the even more congested northbound checkpoint.

One day a pregnant young mother with a handicapped son approached him in the barrio. She had acquired a small sliver of land on the condition that she build a home on it, but she had no money. She asked him if he would build a shelter for her family. He said yes. With the help of a friend, he purchased enough 2x4s, plywood sheets and tar paper to construct a one-room hut with a dirt floor.

One request led to another, and another, until over the next two decades thousands of identical homes were built for destitute families, thousands of American teenagers wielding handsaws and hammers were exposed to third-world poverty and cross-cultural missions, and thousands of miles were put on the missionary's pick-up, so often loaded with 2x4s, plywood sheets and tar paper.

Then another woman approached him. She had been dispatched by her husband to ask the missionary if he would give them his truck. After he realized she was not joking, he told her he would pray about it. Then he drove home, opened his well-worn Bible to one of its dirtiest pages, and read a verse he had taught countless others over the years: "Give to the one who asks you, and do not turn away from the one who wants to borrow from you" (Matthew 5:42). He thought of all the reasons why giving away his truck made no sense. It held sentimental value to him because it once belonged to his father. And it was an indispensable ministry resource, transporting him and his supplies to bare scraps of land claimed by homeless families. Yet the command of Jesus came with no disclaimers.

The next morning, the missionary drove his truck to Tijuana for the last time. He told the woman that he had decided to give her family his truck. Mouth agape, she ran to tell her husband, and the missionary waited, keys in hand. On the horizon he saw the man, walking slowly, head bowed. When they met, the Mexican simply said, eyes still to the ground, "I cannot believe you are doing this for us." The missionary smiled and relinquished his keys without speaking a word.

That evening, after a friend dropped him off at his home, he checked his answering machine. There was a message from someone in Minnesota he had never met. "We would like to donate two vans to your ministry," the voice said. "And, by the way, could you also use a pick-up truck?"

Rare are those who take Jesus at his word, even when it is defies common sense. And blessed are those who witness such radical obedience and who are never again able to say that what Jesus demands is humanly impossible.

What would you be most reluctant to lend or even give away? Can you surrender that possession to God, to be used by him as he wills?

MATTHEW 5:43-45; LUKE 6:27-28

IT'S HARD TO KNOW WHICH WAS MORE SHOCKING TO those who heard the Sermon on the Mount—Christ's command to love their enemies, or the list of ways he told them to do it.

Matthew's unsheddable takeaway was that Jesus expected what no patriotic rabbi had ever dared suggest. After all, to be born a Jew was to inherit enemies. And are not enemies of the Jews also enemies of God? So, the clergy agreed, to hate those who hate God is as much an act of devotion as is loving those who love him.

But Jesus broke ranks. "You have heard that it was said, 'Love your neighbor and hate your enemy.' But I tell you, love your enemies" (Matthew 5:43-44). Jaws dropped, not because what he said was contrary to Scripture, but because it was contrary to culture. What patriotism had obscured, Jesus revived, using God the Father as the prototype: "He causes his sun to rise on the evil and the good, and sends rain on the righteous and the unrighteous" (Matthew 5:45). If God loves indiscriminately, who are we to pick and choose? Matthew could not shake such conviction.

Later, when Luke interviewed those who had been in the audience, he was struck by the details they remembered. Jesus had not only told them what to do, but how to do it:

- "Do good to those who hate you" (Luke 6:27). It's not enough to refrain from revenge; we are to heap upon their head burning coals of kindness. We are to wash the feet of our betrayer and heal the severed ear of our arrestor.
- "Bless those who curse you" (Luke 6:28). Is it not sufficient to endure slander silently? No. To the one who says, "Can anything good come from Nazareth?" we are to effuse praise, saying, "Here is one in whom is no deceit."
- "Pray for those who mistreat you" (Luke 6:28). And no imprecatory prayer, but rather, "Father, forgive them, for they do not know what they are doing," even if the hands stretched out in prayer are stapled to a cross.

A cross. Is that not the supreme icon of love for one's enemies? Remember, it was while we were God's enemies that Christ died for us (Romans 5:8, 10). To bestow sun and rain on the ungrateful and wicked is one thing, but to sacrifice his son for them! For us! How can we, after that, ever justify hatred?

Who has mistreated you most maliciously? How can you be proactive in loving them?

Enemies

LUKE 6:32-35

DEEP OR WIDE? That is the question we ask when we seek clarity about how God wants us to progress from the fundamental responsibility to love our neighbor as ourselves. Does he want us to add depth to our love for co-disciples, or to add breadth by loving even those who do not like us?

The case for depth is irrefutable. When Jesus was preparing his followers to carry on his mission in his absence, he taught them that the key to credibility is mutual self-sacrifice: "By this everyone will know that you are my disciples, if you love *one another*" (John 13:35). The apostle John went even further: "No one has ever seen God, but if we love *one another*, God lives in us" (1 John 4:12). Sure enough, when Christlike love saturated the early church, the Lord added to their number daily those who were being saved (Acts 2:47). No wonder Peter said to Christians who already had sincere love for each other, "Love *one another* deeply, from the heart" (1 Peter 1:22).

And yet, depth is never an excuse for lack of breadth. "If you love those who love you," Jesus asked, "what credit is that to you? Even sinners love those who love them. And if you do good to those who are good to you, what credit is that to you? Even sinners do that. And if you lend to those from whom you expect repayment, what credit is that to you? Even sinners lend to sinners, expecting to be repaid in full" (Luke 6:32-34). There is nothing unusual about in-house love. Mutual back-scratching happens in every fraternal and sororal organization on the planet, secular and religious. Even a church that takes care of its own blends in.

No, if you want to be rewarded by God and respected by adversaries, let the floodwaters of your love overflow the banks of your tribe. Let it spread out recklessly and indiscriminately. Let it drench even those who marginalize, malign and mistreat you.

Who has disrespectfully dismissed you because of your faith? What action can you take to honor them?

Who has damaged your reputation with others by saying things behind your back that are untrue? What can you say about them that is both true and kind?

Who has wounded you—emotionally, physically or financially? How can you do to them what you wish they would do to you?

Why does Jesus ask so much? Because "then your reward will be great" (Luke 6:35). Heavenly treasures await those who love like this.

More importantly, it is this kind of love that makes God look good. When you love those who least deserve it, Jesus said, "you will be children of the Most High, because he is kind to the ungrateful and wicked" (Luke 6:35). If memory serves, we were as ungrateful and wicked as everyone else before Jesus gave up his life to make us his friends. Greater love—and greater influence—has no one than the one who lives (or dies) like this.

Deep or wide? It's not either/or. It's both/and.

What "enemy" is the Spirit of God leading you to love? How can you begin to do it today?

MATTHEW 5:48; LUKE 6:36

"Be perfect," Jesus said, "as your heavenly Father is perfect" (Matthew 5:48). How can such words do anything but snuff out our smoldering wick of hope? For all have sinned. Strive as we might, we are doomed to fall short of the glory of God.

Surely, by now, whatever self-confidence we brought to the mount has been extinguished by the sermon we have heard here. We knew murder could cast a person into hell, but anger? And of course God will judge adultery, but lust as well? It's challenging enough to love our neighbors, but what's this? Enemies, too? If we have to be perfect to inherit the kingdom of heaven, what chance does any of us have?

Blessed are those who know themselves well enough to despair of achieving perfection, for it is in such poverty of spirit that they are able to receive the kingdom of heaven like a child, rather than asking the rich-spirited question, "What good thing must I do to get eternal life?"

But once we have been declared perfect by our merciful God, how do we become in real life what we now are in his eyes? What is the next step on our Everest climb?

If the answer to that question is veiled by Matthew, it is divulged by Luke, whose careful investigation of what Jesus said yielded a more targeted quote: "Be merciful, just as your Father is merciful" (Luke 6:36). Ah, so this is the perfection Jesus had in mind! It is the perfection that has eyes to see the need fueling the sin and a heart to feel compassion for the lost child inside the costume of a malicious persecutor. It is the perfection that turns the other cheek, pays double what the plaintiff seeks, walks two miles when only one is required, gives to anyone who asks, lends with no expectation of repayment. It is the perfection that does to others—even our enemies—what we would have them do to us.

We know we will not be perfect until we are holy, as God is holy, but isn't it wonderful that between here and there we can love others as he first loved us? Aren't you glad that we are not called to judge or condemn, but to empathize and forgive?

Freely we have received the mercy of God; freely we now re-gift that mercy to others. This is always the next step on our journey toward perfection.

Who needs your mercy as desperately as you needed the mercy of God?

Exhibitionism

Matthew 6:1

How ironic it is that we who seek to do good are insulted by the prospect of heavenly recognition, yet we cannot resist the allure of the earthly alternative.

Why, we would never poison our good deeds with an eye toward rewards! To do what we do with any other motive than the love of Christ is to taint it with selfishness. May we never be guilty of so carnal an incentive!

But if other people happen to see us doing good and applaud us for it, well, how can that be avoided?

Do we know our hearts well enough to admit that, when we are on our best behavior, we are capable of being just conspicuous enough to increase the likelihood that others will notice?

We testify that God has been faithful to meet all our needs as we have brought the whole tithe into the storehouse.

We are asked to close the meeting in prayer, and we hear ourselves speaking to God in ways we never do when no one else is listening.

We quietly decline a menu at the restaurant, and only after others ask us why do we divulge that we are fasting.

We fold a $100 bill into our palm and shake the hand of a friend in need, rather than anonymously sliding it under their door.

The urge to be caught red-handed doing good is so strong that Jesus said it takes intentionality to resist the temptation. "Be careful not to practice your righteousness in front of others to be seen by them," he warned us (Matthew 6:1).

But it is what he said next that discredits our disparagement of heavenly recognition. "If you do, you will have no reward from your Father in heaven." What's this? Jesus, the one who taught us to do everything in love, encouraging the pursuit of heavenly rewards! Why? Is it because we are mercenary disciples who are unlikely to do anything good without knowing what's in it for us? No, it's because we can be led by love and motivated by rewards at the same time. Multiple motives are not the same as mixed motives. Otherwise, why would the one who teaches us to do everything in love mention rewards 10 times in the Sermon on the Mount alone?

Our problem is not that we are motivated by rewards, just that we are motivated by the wrong ones. We forfeit the eternal but seek the fleeting. It's as if we don't really believe that whatever rewards we will receive in heaven will have any effect on our eternal happiness. If erroneous eschatology robs us of all motivation to pursue eternal rewards, despite the promises of Jesus, who can blame us for practicing our righteousness before others to be seen by them? Better to leak our good deeds to the press and get the admiration of our peers than to hide them under a bowl and get nothing at all.

What are you doing, right now, that is earning you no earthly recognition but storing up rewards in heaven?

Giving

Matthew 6:2-4

There is perhaps no truer expression of godliness than sharing with others what we could keep for ourselves—which is precisely why we are tempted to give ostentatiously. For who does not crave the respect of others? And what better virtue to be known for than generosity?

Fund-raising experts know this, which is why churches are littered with plaques, hospital wings are named after philanthropists, and university walkways are paved with engraved bricks. It is why members of golden-whatever clubs are named in brochures and the presidents of non-profits send personal thank-you letters to their biggest donors. If recognition is what it takes to fill the coffers, so be it. It's for a good cause.

Yes, but if our motive for giving is publicity for ourselves rather than pity for the poor, we are merely applause-starved actors, pretending to be more righteous than we really are. Jesus had a label for such people. Hypocrites. Mask-wearers.

If you are going to give, why do it for the measly reward of a momentary attaboy when God offers so much more to those who keep their giving under wraps?

Think about it. Is it better to bask in the admiration of people, or to experience the intrinsic satisfaction Jesus was describing when he said, "It is more blessed to give than to receive" (Acts 20:35)?

Is it better to purchase such fleeting publicity at so high a price, or to give inconspicuously so as not to void the promise that "those who give to the poor will lack nothing" (Proverbs 28:27)?

Is it better to seek earthly honor, with its fast-approaching expiration date, or to lay up for yourself a treasure in heaven that will never fail, where no thief comes near and no moth destroys (Luke 12:33)?

Jesus had immeasurable riches, but he gave so generously that he was reduced to poverty. He did not do it for his own glory but only for our good, so that through his poverty we might become rich. This is the one who says to us: "When you give to the needy, do not announce it with trumpets, as the hypocrites do in the synagogues and on the streets, to be honored by others. Truly I tell you, they have received their reward in full. But when you give to the needy, do not let your left hand know what your right hand is doing, so that your giving may be in secret. Then your Father, who sees what is done in secret, will reward you" (Matthew 6:2-4).

When we give, there is always an audience. But it's up to us to decide the size of that audience. Blessed are those who give for an audience of one.

How can you ensure that your giving in the future will be more secretive than your giving has been in the past?

Prayer

Matthew 6:5-6

ANYONE WHO HAS BEEN PART OF A RELIGIOUS COMMUNITY has endured enough prayer-performances to find the words of Jesus on the subject refreshing. "When you pray," he said, "do not be like the hypocrites, for they love to pray standing in the synagogues and on the street corners to be seen by others. Truly I tell you, they have received their reward in full. But when you pray, go into your room, close the door and pray to your Father, who is unseen. Then your Father, who sees what is done in secret, will reward you" (Matthew 6:5-6). Although we are unqualified to discern the motives of those whose public prayers sound more Shakespearean than spontaneous, we cannot help but wonder who they are trying to impress, and when they will run out of gas.

We want to be different, but it's hard to talk to God as if no one else is listening when, so often, others are listening. Not long after Jesus taught us to pray solitarily, the early church started praying corporately. They joined together constantly in prayer in the days before Pentecost (Acts 1:14). They raised their voices together in prayer to God when Peter and John were released from jail (Acts 4:24). They prayed together earnestly when Peter was imprisoned yet again (Acts 12:5, 12). Paul urged us to lift up holy hands in prayer when we worship together (1 Timothy 2:8). James instructed us to request prayer from church elders when we are sick (James 5:14). How could we be apathetic about eloquence when all our role models pray standing, if not in synagogues and on street corners, at least in places far more public than inner rooms with closed doors?

But look, there, in the distance. Do you see the lone figure, too far from the prayer meeting to be heard? If you have eyes to see, you will spot him often. Sometimes he will be nothing more than a silhouette against a pre-dawn sky (Mark 1:35). At other times his face can be seen at any hour of the night, looking up toward the moonlight (Luke 6:12). You may see be able to catch a glimpse of him ascending a mountain in the dark, alone, so isolated that he could shout to the heavens and not be heard (Matthew 14:23). Or, as you drift in and out of sleep, you might see him, just a stone's throw away, on his knees, his face stained with tears, with sweat, with blood (Luke 22:44).

You may not be able to hear what he is praying. But that is because he is not teaching us what to say, but where to pray. Behind closed doors, outside of town, atop a mountain, in an olive grove—all are fine, as long as we are alone.

If you want to build the kind of prayer habits that will be rewarded by your heavenly Father, do not just listen to Jesus; watch him. Then emulate him. The more often you withdraw to lonely places and pray, the better able you will be to commune with God in the most public of places, indifferent to the scores posted by human judges.

How can you increase the time you spend in solitary prayer without decreasing the time you spend in corporate prayer?

Superstition

MATTHEW 6:7-8

AT THIS MOMENT, ALL AROUND THE WORLD, countless people are trying to talk to God. A well-dressed gentleman with a baritone brogue is standing in a chapel, extolling the immensity of God with a litany of adjectives that is stirring the hearts of his fellow congregants. A bored nun is mumbling the Rosary as her fingers navigate the familiar terrain of her prayer-bead abacus. A man is kneeling face-down on a prayer mat, reciting, in a foreign language, the same prescribed words he prayed at precisely the same time yesterday. A young woman is sitting cross-legged on a hardwood floor, eyes closed, whispering a looping mantra. A shirtless man is shouting to the heavens and flogging his own back with a blood-stained whip.

But conspicuously absent from this discordant din is the word God most wants to hear.

Father.

It feels irreverent for us to address the Sovereign of the universe so informally, for he is so large, and we are so small; he so holy, we so sinful; he so powerful, we so weak. We are at a loss as to how to approach him, and so we do it in many silly and superstitious ways. We did not know how simple it could be until Jesus said: "When you pray, do not keep on babbling like pagans, for they think they will be heard because of their many words. Do not be like them, for your Father knows what you need before you ask him" (Matthew 6:7-8).

Our Father? Yes, as incredible as it sounds, God wants us to call him Dad. We are his children, after all—brothers and sisters of Jesus—each with a distinctive, familiar voice that tickles his ears and touches his heart. And he is as eager as any parent to give his children good gifts, but he is too wise and too protective to ever give us less than the best. What a wonder, and what a comfort, that he knows what we need even before we ask. There are no magic words to memorize, no timecards to punch, no techniques to master. There is just an invitation to come, as we are, and to spill our guts to the one whose affection and compassion are veiled only by his invisibility.

And if we cannot fully express ourselves to him in a few words—if it takes an hour, if it takes all night, if it means returning to him again and again and saying nothing that we have not said before—he has all the time in the world, and nothing better to do. Just don't insult him by thinking that what you say or how long it takes you to say it makes him any more willing to answer.

He could not be more willing. Remember, he's your Father.

What habits, traditions or superstitions do you need to shed in order to talk to your heavenly Father in a way that is natural for you as his son or daughter?

Reverence

Matthew 6:9

His is the most venerable name that has ever crossed our lips, yet the irreverence with which we speak it testifies to our utter ignorance. For if we saw God as he is, both adoration and terror would purge us of our nonchalance.

When Isaiah saw the LORD, surrounded by seraphim who covered their faces as they proclaimed, "Holy, holy, holy is the LORD Almighty," he spluttered: "Woe to me! For I am a man of unclean lips, and my eyes have seen the King, the LORD Almighty." When the Israelites passed through the water-walled hallway of the Red Sea, and then watched the walls collapse upon their Egyptian pursuers, they stood aghast before the LORD. When Mt. Sinai trembled violently, spewing smoke into the lightning-strobed sky, they backed away in terror and begged Moses speak to and for God, for the unfiltered voice of the LORD would surely be unsurvivable.

Would we be any different, we who are undone by house-rattling thunder, we who whimper when ocean waves rage, we who cannot bear to stare into the midnight sky long enough to ponder the implications of its vastness?

And yet this dreadfully immense and unimaginably mighty God is our Father! He is compassionate and gracious, slow to anger, abounding in love and faithfulness. He is close to the brokenhearted and saves those who are crushed in spirit. He tends his flock like a shepherd, gathering us in his arms and carrying us close to his heart. He counts the hairs on our head and bottles the tears we shed. When we return to him after we have strayed, he runs to us and smothers us with hugs and kisses. He quiets us with his love and rejoices over us with singing.

Omnipotent yet intimate! Emitting unapproachable light and yet lavishing unquenchable love! How could we ever speak the name of our God so casually, or, worse, so profanely?

"This is how you should pray," Jesus said (Matthew 6:9): "'Our Father in heaven, hallowed be your name.'"

Yes, may the mention of his name set our hearts on fire and turn our legs to jelly. May we never again take the name of the Lord in vain. May we revere it. May we cherish it. May we honor it. And may our awe of God be so contagious that out of the overflow of unveiled hearts more coal-cleansed mouths will speak the words, "Holy, holy, holy is the Lord Almighty," until the whole earth is full of his glory.

For what attribute or mighty deed do you hallow the name of your Father in heaven today?

Kingdom

Matthew 6:10

Why, after all this time, does the prayer, "Your kingdom come, your will be done, on earth as it is in heaven" (Matthew 6:10) still feel unanswered? Is it not because what we long to see God do all around us must begin within us? And does not history testify that this is where his reign encounters its fiercest resistance?

The Garden of Eden was God's kingdom, briefly. Man and woman, perfect in body and soul, living nakedly before God and one another, seeing, touching, smelling, tasting all the pleasures of heaven on earth. But it was what they heard that did them in. A serpent's whisper that God's one and only prohibition was not protective but restrictive, keeping the secret to an even better life just out of reach. The seed of Satan's word found receptive soil that produced 30, 60, 100 times the mistrust and rebellion that was sown. A flaming sword has kept the tree of life off limits ever since, and the world still decays under the dragon's mutinous rule.

In Noah God saw the potential for a hard reset, but the tower-builders of Babel proved that not even a global flood could eradicate the virus of sin that sheltered in the ark.

If not Noah, then, perhaps Abraham? A brand-new nation, blessed uniquely by God, might be a fountain of life to the whole world! But within two generations the waters of that fountain were too bitter for anyone to acquire a taste for the goodness of the Lord.

Moses revived hope, leading Israel homeward from Egypt via Mt. Sinai, where the possibility of a Shekinah-bright future was chiseled into stone tablets. But, as in Eden, sin proved unrestrainable by law. Whether in the wilderness or in the Promised Land, everyone did what was right in their own eyes.

And then came King David, a man after God's own heart, under whose righteous leadership Israel finally began to look like the kingdom of God. But an illicit affair created a hairline crack that ultimately split one nation into two, and the divided kingdom, deaf to the prophets, could not stand against invading armies.

Yet upon the rubble of so many broken dreams, Jesus revived the inextinguishable hope that the kingdom of God was near. And, instinctively, those who prayed for the coming of that kingdom focused outward, not inward.

Little did they know that their Messiah had come, not to claim acreage, but to eradicate the enemy within. On the cross he removed the sin that had forever sabotaged God's kingdom-building plans. Finally, through those who traded the futility of self-reformation for robes made white by the blood of the Lamb, the kingdom of God began growing—like a mustard seed, like yeast—where the battle is won: within.

We have been graced to live in such a time as this, when a heart of stone can become a heart of flesh, when what was once a stronghold of evil can become an abode of the Holy One.

And yet we must admit that even we are haunted by old habits. Yes, the indwelling Spirit is leading us back to the Garden as we trust and obey, but still we feel unwelcome urges and hear alluring whispers. *You will surely not die.* We so want God's kingdom to come, but there is a residue of rebellion in our flesh.

And so it is that we pray with determined persistence, "Your kingdom come, your will be done, on earth as it is in heaven" (Matthew 6:10). We still long to see the kingdom of the world become the kingdom of our Lord and of his Messiah; but our eyes have been opened to the good and evil in our own soul, and so we pray, "Not my will, but yours be done."

By what fleshly passion are you most relentlessly haunted? How persistently are you battling this temptation with the prayer, "Not my will, but your will be done"?

Provision

MATTHEW 6:11

As the sun rises, the birds of the air begin gathering their daily provisions, and anxious humans wake to a new day of sowing, reaping and storing away in barns.

A father lectures his teenage son on the importance of hard work, warning him that if he does not provide for himself and his family, no one else will do it for him.

A college freshman settles for the more sensible major, the one that virtually guarantees prosperity, because to pursue the dream that seems to have been planted in her heart by God himself might not pay the bills.

A young couple makes their bi-weekly deposit into a high-yield savings account. Unable to both tithe and save, they have pledged to give God everything except their money, for surely he understands that they must be prudent if they are to survive the inevitable, unpredictable storms of life.

A middle-aged executive diversifies his portfolio to reduce the risk that he may lose the gains he has made managing his investments so shrewdly.

A woman nearing retirement shovels the maximum allowable into her 401k, fearing that her steady savings through the decades will run dry when she needs it most, and then what will she do?

These are among the people who pray, "Give us this day our daily bread" (Matthew 6:11). What a poignant petition it is when it rises from the trusting, dependent hearts of those who will not eat today unless God answers their prayer, but how can those with well-stocked pantries and rainy-day funds utter these words with integrity?

There is a way, if we are willing to accept it. We can give so much away that, if God does not re-fill the jar we have emptied, we have no contingency plan. If Jesus was a financial adviser, this is the advice he would give his clients. He would invite those who have more than enough to be channels of divine provision to those who have less than enough. Such radical generosity equalizes the distribution of God's blessings and breathes living faith into the dry bones of self-sufficiency.

But do we really believe that God's mercies will be as new every morning as manna in the wilderness? Do we dare obey the surprising instinct to share a larger portion of what common sense tells us to save? Are we willing to bet the farm that our heavenly Father will meet our every need if we seek first his kingdom? Or will we who have been created to sing like birds opt instead to race with rats?

How can you exercise such liberal generosity today that you are literally dependent on God for daily bread?

Forgiveness

MATTHEW 6:12

YOU HAVE MET THE PRE-REQUISITE. You have scoured your heart and forgiven your debtors, all of them. Those who betrayed you, misjudged you, excluded you, slandered you, cursed you, abused you—what were their offenses against you, a fellow sinner, compared to your offenses against the Holy One? Denarii to talents, silver coins to bags of gold. If you know your heart at all, you know you have forgiven them.

And now you are praying as the Lord taught you to pray, "Forgive us our debts, as we also have forgiven our debtors" (Matthew 6:12). But you do not feel forgiven.

The fact of it you do not doubt. You were guilty, he was innocent, yet he paid the debt you owe. The lamb without blemish was sacrificed. The gavel has dropped. The curtain is torn.

So why do you still feel scarlet shame rather than snow-white innocence? Why does the guilt of your transgressions follow you from east to west? Why do iniquities that were hurled into the depths of the sea rise again to haunt you?

Is it because your repentance was not tearful enough?

Is it because of that time you returned to your folly, like a dog returns to its vomit?

Is it because your soul is harboring bitterness so deep that your conscious mind cannot find it, let alone evict it?

Is it because your faith is counterfeit, confirming to you by its inability to dispel the darkness that you are still in your sins?

No, dear child of God. It is because you have a ruthless enemy who knows that your most exploitable vulnerability is a sensitive conscience. Guilt and shame are the weapons of his warfare. They were no match for grace and truth, but now he hopes that perhaps they are strong enough to rob you of the joy of your salvation. For who is so bold as to beckon others out of Satan's dark dungeon if it is not one who has found freedom exhilarating?

You feel like a powerless victim, but you are not. You are a wounded warrior who, though bloodied by battle, still wears the full armor of God. The belt of divine truth. The breastplate of Christ's righteousness. The cleats of the peace-with-God gospel. The accusation-deflecting shield of faith. The secure helmet of salvation. And you still wield the mighty sword of the Spirit. Speak aloud the apt word of God at the right time, and the father of lies will flee from you. This is your superpower, and this is your birthright. For deeper than all doubts, and impervious to all attacks, is the truth that you—yes, you—are, now and forever, forgiven.

For what do you feel unforgiven? What does the word of God say about that feeling?

Temptation

MATTHEW 6:13

WHO CAN KNOW HOW INTENSELY JESUS SUFFERED when he was led into temptation? How much strength does it take for a perfect human being to endure an assault more precise and prolonged than any before or since? What could be so alluring that 40 days of fasting and prayer were needed for the Son of God to resist? How ferocious was the lion in the desert that, when he finally relented, angels were summoned to help our Lord recover?

Whatever Jesus experienced in the wilderness, it was so unspeakably agonizing that he taught his disciples to pray, "Lead us not into temptation, but deliver us from the evil one." (Matthew 6:13). The one in whose steps we are called to follow, even to the point of taking up a cross, advises us to beg for this one exception. Anything but facing the devil alone.

But do we grasp the prowess of our adversary—or the fragility of our willpower—fully enough to cry out for such deliverance? Or do we think so lowly of him and so highly of ourselves that we feel up to the challenge? After all, no temptation will ever overtake us except what is common to humanity. And our faithful God will never let us be tempted beyond what we can bear. No, when we are tempted, he will provide a way out so that we can stand up under it. Why, all we need to do to resist the devil is to approach God's throne of grace confidently, for we will surely receive mercy and find grace to help us in our time of need.

Such emergency measures are indispensable, but if we think we can conquer temptation routinely, we have been poisoned with the same pride that brought down David, the man after God's own heart, doomed by a single lustful look at an unguarded moment. We share the hubris of Peter, too sleepy to watch and pray, doing the unthinkable three times before the rooster crowed.

How many of our role models must become casualties, and how many times must we ourselves fall, before we realize that we are one spectacular failure away from becoming a cautionary tale? How long will we keep strolling past the harlot's house at dusk before we come to our senses and beg God to lead us not into temptation?

The only sure deliverance from the evil one for mortals like us is not to fight, but to flee. Our heavenly Father wants to lead us to safety. The fact that part of us doesn't want to go there is a given. The flesh is weak, but is the spirit willing?

What kind of temptation are you most susceptible to? Are you praying daily that God will lead you in the opposite direction?

MATTHEW 6:14-15

"IF YOU FORGIVE other people when they sin against you, your heavenly Father will also forgive you. But if you do not forgive others their sins, your Father will not forgive your sins" (Matthew 6:14-15). Which is more shocking: the absence of sympathy in Christ's words, or the unorthodox theology in them?

The last thing we want to hear if we have been deeply hurt by others is a sulfuric warning against bitterness. The pain of betrayal is excruciating. We long for an empathetic ear and a loyal embrace. We need permission to grieve, to simmer, to erupt. Maybe the day will come when we can forgive, but not today. It is too soon. The wound is too deep. *Just be quiet and let me vent.*

But Jesus has no patience for wound-licking or grudge-holding. If anyone has the right to keep a record of wrongs, it is God. So, if he doesn't, how can we? Of course it stung. It still does. But commiseration will do us no good. The only balm is forgiveness. So, choose it, Jesus says. Now.

And if we nurse resentment instead? Jesus' words are un-misunderstandable. As we have, or have not, forgiven our debtors, God will, or will not, forgive us.

What are we to do with that? No one else has ever told us that God's forgiveness of our sins is conditioned upon our forgiveness of others' sins against us. No, he forgives us first, and we follow suit. "Forgive as the Lord forgave you" (Colossians 3:13).

Is this not the progression Jesus himself taught in the parable of the unmerciful servant? The servant is hopelessly indebted to the king. He drops to his knees and begs for patience. Instead, he gets mercy. The king cancels his debt.

But from the palace the servant beelines to the home of one who owes him far less. He shoves his debtor against the wall, puts his hands around his neck and demands immediate repayment. The debtor drops to his knees and begs for patience. Instead, he gets jail time. Only when the debt is paid will he be released.

Appalled informants brief the king. He is enraged. "Shouldn't you have had mercy on your fellow servant just as I had on you?" he says—and then he does what we cannot imagine God ever doing: he rescinds his forgiveness. The heartless servant is incarcerated and, until full repayment is made, he is tortured. Yes, tortured.

Then, with the same sternness as he exhibited in the Sermon on the Mount, Jesus stated the unthinkable: "This is how my heavenly Father will treat each of you unless you forgive your brother or sister from your heart" (Matthew 18:35).

How sobering that the grace of God that flooded into our repentant heart—all the joy and peace that the erasure of our past and a reunion with God elicits—can be confiscated in a moment.

Jesus was determined to deliver us from such torture. No wonder there was no tenderness in his warning against bitterness. Better to wound his friends than to blow them kisses as they descend into the dungeon.

Who have you not forgiven from the heart? What is preventing you from doing so right now?

Matthew 6:16-18

WE WHO WORSHIP JESUS AS GOD sometimes forget that he was also a man. How much of what he did do we wrongly attribute to his unattainable deity rather than to his exemplary humanity? Did he not demonstrate what is possible for a mere human, rightly related to God?

The gospel writers made no mention of Christ's divine power when they described his victory over the devil in the wilderness. Instead, they focused on his spiritual preparation. He fasted for 40 days. If our Lord and Teacher was so hungry for God the Father that he skipped that many meals to seek him, is there any question that fasting will benefit us as well?

Not to Jesus. In his Sermon on the Mount, he began his instructions on the topic, not with the phrase "If you fast..." but "When you fast..." (Matthew 6:16). He affirmed the practice not only because he was aware of how many times in history those who fasted received God's comfort, guidance, and grace, but also because he himself, after emptying himself of independent omnipotence, had received a 40-day transfusion of supernatural strength.

All the rewards of fasting are available to us as well, on one condition: that we resist the urge to tell others we are doing it.

"When you fast," Jesus said, "do not look somber as the hypocrites do, for they disfigure their faces to show others they are fasting. Truly I tell you, they have received their reward in full. But when you fast, put oil on your head and wash your face, so that it will not be obvious to others that you are fasting, but only to your Father, who is unseen; and your Father, who sees what is done in secret, will reward you" (Matthew 6:16-18).

How well Jesus knows us! The more we deny our flesh, the more determined it is to find an outlet. *So, you're going to pray instead of eating? That's impressive! You must find a way to let others know.* And we do. We may not announce it with trumpets, we may not stand in the temple and pray aloud about our fasting schedule, we may not "try to look miserable and disheveled" (Matthew 6:16, NLT), but we find discreet ways to draw attention to our devotion, convincing ourselves that we have legitimate reasons to ignore the clear warning of Jesus. Then we wonder why God does not dispense what we have given up so many calories to seek.

Or we resist the urge to gather an audience, instead fasting as inconspicuously as possible. That is when the heavens open and God comes near to give us the desire of our heart, and we learn that man does not live on bread alone, but on every word that comes from the mouth of God.

What do you want from God more than food? How can you fast and pray without anyone but him noticing?

Investments

Matthew 6:19-20

If there is anything more remarkable than the fact that we can make heavenly investments with earthly resources, it is that so few of us choose to do so. This, despite our claim to believe in Jesus.

"Do not store up for yourselves treasures on earth, where moths and vermin destroy, and where thieves break in and steal," he said to rich and poor alike. "But store up for yourselves treasures in heaven, where moths and vermin do not destroy, and where thieves do not break in and steal" (Matthew 6:19-20).

The afterlife is a midnight fog to us, but we know it is noonday bright to Jesus. We do not doubt that his eternal perspective gives him wisdom that no one whose days are numbered can match. Yet when he advises us to invest in that which pays dividends not before but after death, we default to what we know. We endeavor to make our seventy or eighty years as luxurious as possible before we finish our years with a moan and fly away. Our ambition is to earn more, save more, buy more, collect more, use more, because if heaven is as great as Jesus says it is, why not enjoy our treasures down here where they actually make a difference in our quality of life?

But where did we get the idea that heaven will be equally pleasurable to everyone who goes there? Certainly not from Jesus. To the contrary, he taught that every choice we make today will matter forever. You and I have an earthly treasury and a heavenly one, and every deposit we make is an either/or decision. You can enjoy it now or enjoy it forever, not both. Who among us has ears to hear?

Some do. There are outliers in our midst who have set their hearts on pilgrimage. They do not stand out except to seem oddly content despite their modest trappings. How quietly they feed the hungry, clothe the naked, welcome strangers, visit prisoners. Their left hand does not notice their right hand selling possessions and giving to the poor. Far from vacation resorts they eat with outcasts and welcome children in Jesus' name. Their marketable talents are squandered on those who cannot afford to pay. While others rise to the top, they wash the feet of the saints. It is as if everything they do with their money, time and know-how is done with no ambition whatsoever.

Perhaps. Or perhaps they are as ambitious as the rest of us— but more far-sighted. Jonathan Edwards resolved "to endeavor to obtain for myself as much happiness, in the other world, as I possibly can, with all the power, might, vigor, and vehemence, yea violence, I am capable of." To pursue instead treasures that will be destroyed by vermin or stolen by thieves only makes sense if Jesus was wrong.

How have you, in faith, stored up treasures in heaven? What radical changes can you make now to improve your investment strategy?

Treasure

Matthew 6:21

"Where your treasure is, there your heart will be also," Jesus said (Matthew 6:21). But we process his words dyslexically. We think he is simply echoing the proverbial warning to guard our heart, for out of it flow the issues of life. Be careful what you fixate on, for that is what you will invest in.

That may be true, but it is not what Jesus said. He did not teach that our expenditures reveal our affections. He taught something far less abstract, something disturbingly practical: our expenditures shape our affections.

The heart is not a wild beast with a mind of its own. It is not the master of our fate. It is the product of our choices—as strong as a cable to be sure, but spun from thousands of decisions, every dollar a wire.

We are not to wait for the inspirational urge to sell our possessions and give to the poor; we are to simply do it. And when we do, we not only store up treasure in heaven; we adrenalize the anticipation of going there. Every meal we serve, every thirst we quench, every garment we share sets our heart on things above, for the stranger we shelter, the patient we nurse, the prisoner we visit is the same Jesus who will one day welcome us home. We cannot but thrill at the thought that by being kind to the poor we are lending to the LORD, and that he will reward us for what we have done. When we use worldly wealth to make friends who will welcome us into eternal dwellings, we are being more shrewd than the people of this world, because the one whose property we are stewarding faithfully now will one day give us property of our own—and how could our heart not beat with expectancy about the true riches we will receive on that day?

Others may object that it is hypocritical to store up treasures in heaven when our heart is earthbound. Why invest in what we couldn't care less about? Because it's what we invest in that determines what we care most about. "We must store our wealth above," Alfred Plummer wrote, "in order that our hearts may be drawn upwards." And once our heart has been drawn upwards by the force of our will, once it has been trained to beat for eternity, it becomes the wellspring that gushes wisdom on all the issues of life.

What financial investments have you made that will yield eternal profits?

Vision

Matthew 6:22-23

No two people have identical eyesight, not even when they are looking at the same stimuli with perfectly functioning corneas, retinas, and optic nerves—for the process that transforms light into images is more than physiological. It is also spiritual.

"The eye is the lamp of the body," Jesus said (Matthew 6:22). It is not only the window through which light gets in; it is also the torch that illuminates—indeed, determines—what is hidden in our deepest inner recesses. "If your eyes are healthy, your whole body will be full of light. But if your eyes are unhealthy, your whole body will be full of darkness. If then the light within you is darkness, how great is that darkness!" (Matthew 6:22-23).

If you have eyes of greed, if everything you see is either rejected or welcomed based on its monetary value or profit potential, what piles up in the broken cistern of your heart? Abandoned treasures—moth-eaten, rust-eroded, time-cursed.

If you have eyes of lust that see people as objects, existing only for the sake of your sensual appetites, what is your soul if not a red-light district, inhabited by the willing holograms of the most beautiful people you have studied, not only on paper and screen, but also at work, in church, next door?

If you have eyes of pride, forever comparing yourself to others, measuring your assets against their liabilities, your body is but a trophy room, filled with hollow plastic statuettes, foil coated, reflecting the flickers of a dying flame.

But if you have healthy eyes, what kind of kingdom do they create within you? A sunlit garden filled with friends. There is the five-time divorcee whose thirst was finally quenched with living water. And the unrefined fisherman, once so hot-headed, now laughing and telling stories to a circle of friends. The woman out of whom seven demons had come—she is there too, smiling peacefully. Sitting next to her, dressed and in his right mind, is a man once tormented by a herd of spirits. A Pharisee is sharing a meal with a tax collector. No one is there who is blind, deaf or mute. No lepers or epileptics or paralytics. But there are children. Oh so many children.

All of them once passed in front of the gaze of others, but poor vision prevented them from being seen. It was not a blindness of the eyes, but of the heart.

Who, or what, have you seen in the last 24 hours? Who, or what, will you see in the next 24 hours?

Money

MATTHEW 6:24

INSIST AS WE MIGHT THAT MONEY IS NEUTRAL, as likely to be used for good as for evil, we cannot in good conscience appeal to Jesus, for if there was anything that was inherently unrighteous in his eyes, it was Mammon.

Among its myriad dangers, money can turn seemingly benign ambition into metastasizing idolatry. "No one can serve two masters," Jesus said to those who thought it possible to devote themselves to the simultaneous pursuits of God and wealth. "Either you will hate the one and love the other, or you will be devoted to the one and despise the other. You cannot serve both God and money" (Matthew 6:24).

Few would admit to having fallen in love with money, but—here's the test—how do you feel about what Jesus tells you to do with it?

When he says that you cannot be his disciple unless you give up everything you have, what emotions surface? When he tells you to sell your possessions and give to the poor, do you love him for that? When he recommends that, rather than building bigger barns to expand your earthly comfort zone, you deposit your treasures in heaven, what happens inside you? Do you delight to give to everyone who asks you? If someone takes what belongs to you, how strong is the urge to demand it back?

Does it do your heart good to hear Jesus bless those who are poor and hungry, promising to satisfy them in the kingdom of God? Or does your stomach growl when he pronounces woes on the rich and well-fed, warning them of future hunger? Remember the story Jesus told of the man who lived in luxury, numb to the suffering of the beggar at his gate? He found himself in the flames of hell, an uncrossable chasm separating him from the beggar in heaven. Are you looking forward to this reversal of fortunes?

You know that Jesus was talking about money when he said that what is highly valued by people is detestable in God's sight. You know that he warned us to guard against greed, for life does not consist in an abundance of possessions. You know that he said it is easier for a camel to go through the eye of a needle than for a rich person to enter the kingdom of God. But how do you feel about these words?

The more we love money, the greater the temptation to deflect what Jesus taught about it. It is easier to add disclaimers than it is to let his words impact us with full force. But it is far better, if we despise his teachings about money, to admit it now, so that we can repent of our love of Mammon—and hatred of God—before it is too late.

Are you in any way avoiding the teachings of Jesus about money? If so, what would change if you let them sink in?

Worry

MATTHEW 6:25-26, 28-32

THOSE WHO LOVE MONEY are not the only ones in danger of being consumed by it. So too are those whose servitude to money is fueled, not by greed, but by fear. Jesus could see it on the sunbaked faces of so many in the crowd that day. Their furrowed brows and faraway eyes touched his heart, for he knew that they would never taste fine wine, nor rub their bellies after a lavish feast, nor feel luxurious fabric against their skin. Theirs was a day-to-day life, each morning a new struggle for daily bread, each night another bout with anxiety. In a world so indifferent to their needs, even to the needs of their children, how could they not worry?

And yet that's exactly what Jesus forbade. "I tell you, do not worry about your life, what you will eat or drink; or about your body, what you will wear," he said. "Is not life more than food, and the body more than clothes?" (Matthew 6:25). Yes—so much more!—but angst that what God has provided today will be lacking tomorrow sucks the joy out of life, reducing us to nail-biting survivalists.

How Jesus longs for us to know that we are the apple of our Father's eye. The compassion we feel toward our children is but a hint of God's heart toward us. His love for us, and his commitment to meeting—no, to exceeding—our needs is inscribed in creation itself. We need only open our eyes, Jesus said. "Look at the birds of the air; they do not sow or reap or store away in barns, and yet your heavenly Father feeds them." And then, this: "Are you not much more valuable than they?" (Matthew 6:26). If his eye is on the sparrow, can there be any doubt that he is watching you?

"And why do you worry about clothes? See how the flowers of the field grow. They do not labor or spin. Yet I tell you that not even Solomon in all his splendor was dressed like one of these." No textile designer has ever matched on fabric what God has done with flora. "If that is how God clothes the grass of the field, which is here today and tomorrow is thrown into the fire, will he not much more clothe you—you of little faith?" (Matthew 6:28-30). If this was a rebuke, surely it was one dripping with compassion. Jesus was not angry at worrywarts. He pitied them. A thousand yesterdays of God's faithfulness, and they still fretted about tomorrow as if they were alone in the universe.

Are we so different? If anything, our needs seem more daunting. We are obsessed not with daily bread but with monthly bills. A mortgage. Medical insurance. Utilities. Fuel prices. And our long-term goals are overwhelming. College expenses. Retirement income. Life insurance. Inheritance. How can we not fear the future?

Jesus understands. He saw your face in the crowd when he said, "Do not worry, saying, 'What shall we eat?' or 'What shall we drink?' or 'What shall we wear?' For the pagans run after all these things, and your heavenly Father knows that you need them" (Matthew 6:31-32). Do you really think that he who did not spare his own son, but gave him up for you, will not also, along with him, graciously give you everything you need, every single day for the rest of your life? To fear anything less is to forfeit the peace that is your birthright as a beloved child of the God who owns everything.

When has God failed to provide you with all the food, drink and clothing you needed? Why do you fear that tomorrow will be different than all of your yesterdays?

MATTHEW 6:33

How many disciples of Jesus decline the invitation to spend their days and years in the bullseye of their giftedness because they think they cannot afford to do so? They dream big but do little because it doesn't pencil.

Not only does such pragmatism undermine the advance of the kingdom of God; it also turns His children into functional heathen. Did not Jesus say that pagans run after the very things that our heavenly Father promises to give us? When he added the words, "But seek first his kingdom and his righteousness, and all these things will be given to you as well" (Matthew 6:33), he was not making a conditional promise, assuring us that if our priorities are right God will provide for us. No, the provision is ours as an unconditional gift from the one to whom we are much more valuable than birds or wildflowers. It is not that we must either put his kingdom first or provide for ourselves; rather, we can put his kingdom first because divine provision is already promised to us.

What an opportunity! Ever since you first dreamed of leveraging your skills and passions to make a difference in the world, you have longed to cast off restraint. What if you took the risk that Jesus was right about everything? What if you went all in on whatever it is that you suspect God put you on this planet to do? What if you walked away from your professional trajectory, your family's expectations, your pension plan, your investment portfolio, your slavery to keeping up with the Joneses—what if you chucked it all and followed Jesus into the adventure of a lifetime? Those who do so will never be forsaken and their children will never beg for bread.

But look beside the path that Jesus walked. Do you see all the stationary doubters with a death wheel of questions spinning in their heads? *How will I pay the rent? Will our children go to bed hungry? If my ministry is a bust, will I be able to return to my old job? Can I bear to live with less? Will we look pathetic to others? Will I ever be able to retire? What if God leaves us in the lurch?* They did more than count the cost; they looked back, contemplating how difficult it would be to say goodbye to creature comforts and face the prospect of having nowhere to lay their heads. By the time they made up their mind, Jesus had disappeared over the horizon in search of those who at his beckon would gladly leave everything to follow him.

Today, if you hear his voice, do not let your heart be hardened by something so trivial as money. There is a pearl of great value for sale, and for the bargain price of everything you have, it can be yours.

What prevents you from seeking first the kingdom of God?

Compartmentalization

MATTHEW 6:33

THE HARDEST PLACE IN THE WORLD to build the kingdom of God is within your own heart.

When you heeded the call of Jesus to "seek first his kingdom and his righteousness," (Matthew 6:33), you felt inner resistance to his reign immediately. You wondered how you could ever be used by God to advance his kingdom when there was such a glaring gap between who you were in Christ and who you were in real life. *Who am I to tell anyone else how to live?* you asked. Finally, you realized that if you waited until you were perfect to offer yourself as a conduit of God's love and power to others, you would be permanently paralyzed. In fear and trembling you ventured into a world so desperately in need of what God had given you to share, inadequate as you were.

Before long you were marveling at what the Spirit of God could do through such an unlikely disciple. Even as you engaged in daily combat with your flesh, the risks you took in the lives of others bore intoxicating fruit. The lost were found. The broken were healed. The guilty were forgiven. The lonely were loved. You—of all people—were helping to change the world.

At what point did your ambition for kingdom-building eclipse your pursuit of righteousness? When did you lose your appetite for God's word? Your discipline in prayer? Your zeal for purity? When did you begin to rationalize your anger? Your adultery? Your addiction? When did you become a workaholic to avoid the still small voice of God?

The great lie of Christian activism is that what we do matters more than who we are. But you know better, don't you? You know that God is not ignoring your unrighteousness because he deems your ministry indispensable. You know that he will bring your every deed into judgment, including every hidden thing, be it secret motives, whispered words or locked-door indulgences. You know how God detests hypocrisy.

You also know—if you believe what you have preached to others—that no confessed sin is unforgivable and no backsliding is irreversible. Resistance to repentance is so exhausting and so illogical considering the grace that will flood your soul when you simply acknowledge the truth: you are, as you have always been, a sinner in need of a Savior, and you need, now as much as ever, the gift of righteousness that Jesus died to give you. This is the time to seek first his righteousness. Pay heed to the kingdom of God within you, and watch his kingdom grow all around you, to the glory of his grace.

What kingdom-building activities do you need to put on hold in order to seek first God's righteousness?

MATTHEW 6:27, 34

NOT EVERYTHING JESUS SAID WAS PROFOUND. We may imagine him to be an otherworldly figure who spoke mysteries inaccessible to the unenlightened. But sometimes what came out of the depth of the riches of the wisdom and knowledge of the Son of God was nothing more than common sense. For example, there is this rhetorical question: "Can any of you by worrying add a single hour to your life?" (Matthew 6:27). The most famous sermon in history, a message for the ages, and the Messiah states the obvious? How did such a trivial truism make the final cut?

And there is more where that came from. "Each day has enough trouble of its own" (Matthew 6:34). No one got goose bumps when Jesus said that.

But love is not proud. It will stoop as low as necessary to tell us what we need to hear. And who among us does worry about tomorrow despite the knowledge that it will do us no good? We can quote Philippians 4:6-7 and 1 Peter 5:7 by memory, but we fret anyway. Though God's peace is available to those who cast their anxiety on him, our hearts pound and our minds spin as we choose to panic rather than to pray. Among God's new mercies every morning is a day's worth of serenity, but worry races ahead into tomorrow, and manna turns to maggots.

How hard it is to live life in daily increments, and yet this is the rhythm of nature. Yesterday is unchangeable yet blood-bleached. Tomorrow is an adventure that will unfold in God's time, regardless of our impatience or reluctance. But this is the day the Lord has made, and every minute matters. There is stunning beauty to behold, fresh air to inhale, daily bread to taste. If you are fully present, both tears and laughter will come. Listen to the quiet, and you may hear the whisper of God. If your heart and hands are poised to love, surely you will feel the Spirit's nudge. As you do what you know is right and flee what you know is wrong, divine power will course through your veins. Even suffering will be endurable because of the companionship of the one who understands like no one else. So rejoice and be glad in the once-in-a-lifetime gift of today. And "do not worry about tomorrow, for tomorrow will worry about itself" (Matthew 6:34).

There he goes again, serving up the obvious. But imagine building your life on every obvious thing Jesus said! Wisdom is not measured, and joy is not released, by how much we know, but by how much of what we know we do.

What are you worried about? How is your anxiety about what might happen tomorrow affecting your life today?

Judging

Matthew 7:1-2

THERE IS NOTHING AS TERRIFYING as the realization that our God is a consuming fire, nor anything more relieving than the promise that Jesus will shield us from the flames.

Is this not why he came? To expose our guilt and to warn of us of judgment, yes, but then to secure for us a full pardon at the cost of his own life! How could this love that absorbed the raging wrath that we deserve not melt our hearts? And how could mercy's triumph over judgment not forever change our posture toward others whose sins we know to be offensive to God and, increasingly, offensive to us? If Jesus does not condemn them, what else can we say but, "Neither do I condemn you"?

But self-righteousness is a relentless cancer. We may have wept with gratitude for the miracle of grace when we knew how wretched, pitiful, poor, blind, and naked we were. But, ironically, sanctification can make us sanctimonious. Out of the same mouth we praise God for not treating us as our sins deserve and curse people for not measuring up to our standards. We know we will not be judged, yet we become judges, criticizing and condemning others for behavior that is rooted in the very same depravity that once poisoned our own soul.

What we do not consider up there on our high horse is that the guilty verdicts we render will not make the Day of Judgment any worse for them, only for us. "Do not judge," Jesus said, "or you too will be judged. For in the same way you judge others, you will be judged, and with the measure you use, it will be measured to you" (Matthew 7:1-2).

Such words are so disorienting, so alarming, that we tend to deflect them. We cannot imagine any scenario in which, after God has lavished his grace upon us, he would take any of it back. Surely once his gavel drops, our fate is fixed, right? If we cannot rely on the unchangeability of God, all solid ground turns to soup.

But is the parable of the unmerciful servant unambiguous? Did not Jesus teach that the king will withdraw forgiveness from the unforgiving and instead torture them (Matthew 18:34-35)? Did not James echo Jesus when he wrote that judgment without mercy will be shown to anyone who is not merciful (James 2:13)?

We may think it unkind for Jesus to warn us of the lingering possibility of judgment, but it is grace upon grace, for no one knows better than he does what a dreadful thing it is, once we have tasted the heavenly gift, to fall into the hands of the living God.

Whom do you need to stop judging?

Recompense

Luke 6:37-38

How stubbornly simplistic we are in our vision of eternity! All have sinned, but those who repent and believe in Jesus will go to heaven, where for all eternity they will experience identical bliss, regardless of their behavior on earth. Those who reject Christ will be cast into hell, where the fury of God's wrath will be equally agonizing for everyone. What more is there to say?

Such erroneous clarity has many consequences, not the least of which is that it makes obedience optional. There is no reward to be gained by how we live, and no repercussion to be avoided. We obey Jesus voluntarily out of gratitude for his grace. Mercy has triumphed over judgment in our case, so we do not play the judge in the lives of others. We do not condemn them because we know there is no condemnation for us who are in Christ Jesus. We forgive those who have wounded us just as in Christ God has forgiven us. Freely we have received, so freely we give. And if we fail to imitate God in these ways, it may damage his reputation, but it certainly will not alter our eternal quality of life.

No? Then why did Jesus say, "Do not judge, and you will not be judged. Do not condemn, and you will not be condemned. Forgive, and you will be forgiven. Give, and it will be given to you. A good measure, pressed down, shaken together and running over, will be poured into your lap. For with the measure you use, it will be measured to you" (Luke 6:37-38).

We would call such teaching heretical if anyone other than Jesus said it. But he did say it, and more than we can imagine is at stake, so we dare not let our initial objections coat our hearts with Teflon.

Ponder this. The determination to esteem as image-bearers of God those people who could not be more different from you will ensure that, when you look into the eyes of God on Judgment Day, you will feel nothing but affection. But to the extent that you look down your nose at others, you will one day feel the shame of God's disapproval of you. Yes, even as a Christian.

If, no matter how indefensible you find the conduct of others, you refuse to condemn them as worthy of God's wrath, the Day will come when he, holy though he is, will overlook all of your most regrettable actions. But if you condemn others now, don't expect him to go easy on you then.

If you strangle to death whatever bitterness you feel toward those who have hurt you most deeply, God will welcome you home with open arms despite all the ways you have hurt him. But if you hold grudges, so will he.

If your days on earth are marked by generosity toward others, imagine how lavishly God will reward you in heaven. When it seems as if your joy is at full capacity, he will press it down and add more until it spills over the brim and into your lap. But earthly stinginess leads to eternal scarcity.

There's no doubt you're going to heaven. But, believe it or not, the measure of bliss you enjoy there will depend on the measure of grace you dispense here. Jesus said so.

What changes does the Spirit of God want you to make now so that he can reward you more richly later?

LUKE 6:39-40

FEW DECISIONS IN LIFE are as consequential as our choice of teachers because, in the end, we are not shaped by their words so much as we are by their lives. Long after we have forgotten everything they said, the imprint of their example remains, unerasable in our thoughts and replicated in our behavior.

Jesus warned us not to assume the mantle of a teacher—for who wants to be responsible to God not only for their own actions but also for the copycat deeds of their students? No matter how hard a teacher might try to deflect imitation, it is a hazard of the job.

If only teachers were more circumspect. But, no, like carnival barkers, they line the midway through which so many potential disciples meander. Jesus knew how vulnerable shepherdless sheep are, and it compelled him to urge caution. "Can the blind lead the blind?" he asked. "Will they not both fall into a pit? The student is not above the teacher, but everyone who is fully trained will be like their teacher" (Luke 6:39-40).

So, to whom will you entrust the shaping of your life, and on what basis? Their charm? Their fame? Their physical attractiveness? Their pedigree? Their sense of humor? Their self-confidence? Their edginess? It is easy, living as we do in a shallow, entertainment-addicted culture, to obey our infatuations.

But do you have eyes to see beyond image to substance? Have you prayerfully and thoroughly evaluated the character of pastors who pique your interest? Are they who you want to be—not in the eyes of other people, but in the eyes of God? These are vital questions, because whom you choose to call "teacher" is whom you are deciding to become.

What does it tell you about Jesus that he would be so protective of students and so wary of teachers and yet say so authoritatively, "Follow me"? Who do you say he is? The most dangerous of teachers, or the only one worthy of your absolute trust?

It is perfectly natural for us to feel the need for a visible, touchable, relatable teacher, separated as we are by the two millennia between us and Christ. Frederick Buechner said that Jesus is as unknowable as a figure in a scratched and faded newsreel. But if we are determined to take his yoke upon us and learn from him, relegating all other instructors to the status of teaching assistants, does he not emerge from the gospels three-dimensionally, flesh-colored with eyes that sparkle and a voice more familiar than all others? Does not your heart burn when he speaks? Does not the vibrance of his example make all other teachers seem grayscale by comparison? Who else but Jesus would you want to become like?

How are you prioritizing the teachings of Jesus over all other spiritual teachers?

Humility

Matthew 7:3-5

"Why do you look at the speck of sawdust in your brother's eye and pay no attention to the plank in your own eye?" Jesus asked. "How can you say to your brother, 'Let me take the speck out of your eye,' when all the time there is a plank in your own eye? You hypocrite, first take the plank out of your own eye, and then you will see clearly to remove the speck from your brother's eye" (Matthew 7:3-5).

Woe to those who get specks and planks confused. In other words, woe to us—for who is more likely to magnify in others what they minimize in themselves than religious people? How ironic that we follow a man who restored proper proportions to both good and evil, yet when we congregate we are prone to straining out our neighbor's gnats while swallowing our own camels.

Did not Jesus make it unmistakably clear what matters most to God? Love, justice, mercy, humility—these are the virtues that God values, which is why animosity, oppression, indifference and arrogance are so ugly. But these are not the sins we condemn in others. No, we point out more obvious objectionables—the smell of alcohol or tobacco on the breath, an irreligious Sunday morning routine, offensive language, personal pronouns, political affiliation, social media posts, tattoos. We look down our nose at the kind of people Jesus enjoyed the most, oblivious to the fact that we have become the kind of people he enjoyed the least.

Have we so cleaned up the sin in our own camp that we are qualified to criticize others? If so, wouldn't it show in the way we react to behavior we know to be wrong? Would we not approach the sinner personally rather than taking pot shots from the safety of our tribe? And would not sober self-examination precede any corrective overture, lest we miss the plank in pursuit of the speck? And would we not seek to restore the wayward one gently rather than rebuke them harshly, hoping against hope for restoration?

The church is both a blessing and a curse—a blessing to those who seek a band of brothers and sisters to sharpen one another as iron sharpens iron, but a curse to those looking for a lofty perch from which to praise God and with the same tongue curse human beings who bear his image. We are not critics commissioned to judge; we are physicians equipped to heal—but before we can heal others, we must heal ourselves.

What is the biggest plank in your own eye? What can you do today to begin removing it?

Discernment

MATTHEW 7:6

"Do not give dogs what is sacred," Jesus said. "Do not throw your pearls to pigs. If you do, they may trample them under their feet, and turn and tear you to pieces" (Matthew 7:6). While judgmentalism is forbidden, our Lord assured us that discernment is necessary—especially when it comes to sharing that which is most valuable. We have been entrusted with truth far too sacred for some—a pearl, if you will, of great price. To give away such a treasure indiscriminately, to let it fall at the feet of scavengers and swine, is unthinkable.

So it was not surprising that when a Gentile woman came to Jesus and pleaded with him to have mercy on her demon-possessed daughter, he did not answer her a word. "I was sent only to the lost sheep of Israel," he said, not so much to her as to his entourage, and they nodded their agreement that Jews alone merited what the Messiah came to give.

The woman, however, was undeterred. She came closer and knelt before him. "Lord, help me!" she begged.

But Jesus was not about to waste the sacred on the profane. "It is not right to take the children's bread and toss it to the dogs," he said. Those with no appreciation for pedigree may wonder how Jesus could say such a thing, but it drew amens from full-blooded Jews who were grateful that finally their status as God's chosen ones was being respected rather than trodden underfoot.

How they must have sneered at her pitiful reply: "Even the dogs eat the crumbs that fall from their master's table."

Why, then, did Jesus smile? And why did he say, "Woman, you have great faith! Your request is granted"? And why was her daughter healed at that moment? Was it not because Jesus had the discernment to see beyond externals to the heart?

The question is, do we? Or are we like Simon Peter, who heard his once dead, forever alive master say, "Go and make disciples of all nations," yet required the heavenly P.S. "Do not call anything impure that God has made clean" (three times!) before he was willing to step foot into a Gentile household? How many times must we share the secret of eternal life unsuccessfully with our own flesh and blood, how long must we watch them insult the Spirit of grace, before we turn to those who will not treat as an unholy thing the blood of the covenant?

Yes, disciples need discernment—the discernment to see lost children of God where others only see dogs and pigs.

Who, in your circle of acquaintances, have you pre-judged as being disinterested in the gospel?

Expectation

MATTHEW 7:7-8

THE LONGER WE FOLLOW JESUS, the more likely we are to doubt the power of prayer.

In the beginning, were we not astonished by the world of possibilities that Christ's promises unveiled? "Ask and it will be given to you," he said. "Seek and you will find. Knock and the door will be opened to you. For everyone who asks receives; the one who seeks finds; and to the one who knocks, the door will be opened" (Matthew 7:7-8). So we do not live in a closed system in which nothing but human sweat and ingenuity can change our luck! God is at work, listening to the cries of his children and intervening in miraculous ways! These words of Jesus drove us to our knees, and our prayers flew to heaven on the wings of expectation.

But we got mixed results. Yes, sometimes God did exactly what we asked him to do—if not more than we dared ask or even imagine. But there were also times when his answers came in ways we did not expect, and we were disappointed. And, truth be told, there have been heartbreaking times when he has seemed distant and uncaring, despite our faith, despite our persistence, despite our tears. Whether we admitted it or not, his silence in the face our suffering made us wonder if prayer has any power at all. We did not go so far as to say Jesus was wrong, but we could not reconcile his assurances with our experiences.

Well-meaning elders explained to us the many conditions of answered prayer scattered throughout the Scriptures, and with sincerity they asked: *Did you pray in faith? Did you pray in Jesus' name? Did you pray according to God's will? Did you pray with pure motives? Did you pray with no unconfessed sin?* We learned that there are any number of things that might have gone wrong, and we began to add the fine print to our conversations with God.

Let's admit it: Ever so slowly, over time, we have come to expect very little from God, and our flaccid prayers, though biblically precise, testify to our unbelief.

Yes, of course there is more to the truth about prayer than that we can ask God for anything and he will give it to us. That we will find exactly what we seek is simplistic. But whatever else there is to learn about prayer is built on the foundation of this truth: God always opens the door when we knock. He is eager to respond with a perfect blend of love, power, and wisdom.

Perhaps it is time to forget everything else we have been taught about prayer and start over, lest the blade of cynicism whittle the sturdy promise of Jesus down to a powerless twig. This is the thunderous word of God to everyone who has ears to hear: Ask and it will be given to you! Seek and you will find! Knock and the door will be opened! If this truth does not make us want to pray, we need to be born again, again.

What desire of your heart have you stopped asking God to give you?

Fatherhood

Matthew 7:9-11

Whenever Jesus wanted to emphasize God's eagerness to answer our prayers, he did so not by comparing him to exemplary people, but by contrasting him with deficient ones—such as a sleepy neighbor who shares his food only because of the shameless audacity of his friend's midnight door-pounding, or a callous judge who grants a widow justice only to put an end to her relentless badgering. Although Christ's rhetorical device may be foreign to us, we get the point: If persistence can wear down even the most grudging benefactor, imagine the effect it has on our doting father, whose is on the opposite extreme of the generosity spectrum!

But there is one more unsavory character whose wickedness provides a black velvet backdrop upon which to display God's radiance: you. Never one to flatter, Jesus called everyone in attendance at the Sermon on the Mount evil—and if we were there that adjective would fit us as well, wouldn't it? Both our habits and our hearts are works in progress, and much that we think, say and do privately we hope to God will never be known publicly.

But we do get one thing right: we love our kids. At times, that aching affection is our lone redeeming quality. If you are a parent, no doubt your heart's desire is to give your children, not only what they need, but also what they want. To hear them beg for the go-ahead to unwrap your gifts, to see them giddy with joy at what they are holding in their hands, to revel in the pleasure it brings them to play with what cost you so much—well, few things are more satisfying to a dad or a mom. As selfish as we can be, when it comes to our children, we are lavish givers. "Which of you, if your son asks for bread, will give him a stone?" Jesus asked. "Or if he asks for a fish, will give him a snake?" (Matthew 7:9-10). No parent you know would do that. A father would have to be cold-blooded to give his daughter what he knows she least desires. Only a sick or sadistic mother would plug her ears to the cries of her children. No dad or mom would intentionally make the apple of their eye feel unworthy to ask for anything. And yet do we not imagine our heavenly Father to be just such a parent—far less generous to us than we are to our own children?

Not-yet-answered prayer is the petri dish in which such poisonous heresy grows, but temporary circumstances are poor ingredients with which to construct an image of our eternal God. A far better starting point is a self-portrait. "If you, then, though you are evil, know how to give good gifts to your children, how much more will your Father in heaven give good gifts to those who ask him!" (Matthew 7:11). Want proof? Look at the cross. He who did not spare his own son, but gave him up for us all—how will he not also, along with him, graciously give us all things?

Our heavenly Father is immeasurably more open-handed toward us than we are toward our own children. This is a truth that should cleanse us of toxic mistrust in him and fuel persistence in our prayers.

How have you allowed not-yet-answered prayers to deface your image of God?

Love

MATTHEW 7:12

FROM THE BEGINNING OF TIME human beings have longed for simplicity in religion, only to be buried by an avalanche of precepts. How high is the stack, how heavy is the weight, of the laws that have been laid on the backs of those who want to live a life that pleases God? There was a moment in time when it seemed as if everything could be reduced to 10 commandments, but before Moses came down from the sacred mountain the two stone tablets were etched, front and back, with minutia. And even the 248 thou shalts and 365 thou shalt nots of the law failed to cover every detail of life, so generations of rabbis added thousands of additional regulations. Too much was at stake to improvise when it came to appeasing a dangerously holy God.

This was the obsessive-compulsive religion that everyone Jesus met had inherited. How many of those who crowded onto that mountain plateau expected him to put even more laws on the books, and how many hoped against hope for an easier yoke, we don't know, but nothing—not even the words Jesus had spoken moments before—could have prepared them for the revolutionary simplification that came in the form of a single, all-encompassing maxim: "So in everything, do to others what you would have them do to you, for this sums up the Law and the Prophets" (Matthew 7:12).

This Golden Rule so permeates our ethical instincts that we assume Jesus must have been dusting off an adage as old as time. But search through the writings of antiquity and you will find no parallels, except perhaps in the mustard seed, "Love your neighbor as yourself," inconspicuously planted in Leviticus 19 among so many bushels full of prohibitions that it was natural to think of love in negative terms only—not in what we do for others, but in what we refrain from doing to them. In fact, the injunction *Do not do to others what you do not want them to do to you* was practically a cliché—part of pre-Christian ethical and religious texts in China, Egypt, India, Greece, Persia, and, yes, Israel. But Jesus gave love a new definition, not only in the sermon he preached but also in the one he lived. Perhaps no one did anything forbidden to the hemorrhaging woman, to the leper, to the outcast at the well, to the tax collector, to the adulteress, to the madman in the graveyard. But they never felt more loved than they did when Jesus did to them what he would have them do to him.

Do we really want such radical simplicity? Are we prepared to measure our love—for our neighbors and for God too—by what we do rather than by what we do not do? Or, after drinking this new wine, do we prefer the taste of the old?

In the next 24 hours, how can you do for someone else what you would have them do for you?

Salvation

MATTHEW 7:13-14

"ENTER THROUGH THE NARROW GATE," Jesus said. "For wide is the gate and broad is the road that leads to destruction, and many enter through it. But small is the gate and narrow the road that leads to life, and only a few find it" (Matthew 7:13-14). These words would be much more alarming if not for our certainty that we are among that small minority who have threaded the needle.

But do we dare presume that Christ's warning was not meant for us?

How selective has our hearing been since we first heard his voice? Even after he said that anger is murder and lust is adultery and that only the pure in heart will see God, even after he said that we must be perfect as our heavenly Father is perfect, how many of us still lack the poverty of spirit to admit that if we ever see the kingdom of heaven it will only be because of his blood-red grace?

How many of us prayed a prayer, raised a hand, walked an aisle or checked a box half a lifetime ago, believing that such a thin fire-retardant veneer gave us license to return to our folly? Jesus could not have been more clear about the fact that those who do good will rise to live and those who do evil will rise to be condemned, that his angels will weed out of his kingdom all who do evil, that only those who keep his word will never see death—and yet we comfort ourselves with the fantasy that, though we have sown to please the flesh, we will reap eternal life.

How many of us are on the wide, descending road today because we followed Jesus impulsively, underestimating the cost of finishing what we started? When our safety was threatened, the cross became too heavy to bear. When loyalty was tested, friends and family came first. When generosity was commanded, possessions were too precious to relinquish. Like seed sown on rocky soil, we were quick to sprout, but when trouble or persecution came because of the word, we fell away. And even though Jesus said that the love of most would grow cold and that only those who stand firm to the end will be saved, we feel eternally secure. True, we took an early exit from the narrow road, but we can still remember the day we entered through the narrow gate, so of course we will be saved, even if only as those escaping through the flames.

Are you really so sure you are among the select few who are on the road that leads to life? Does your confidence take into account everything Jesus taught, or have you cherry-picked verses that whisper "Peace, peace" to your soul when there is no peace? Jesus loved us too much to gush false assurance, and if we feel wounded by his words, it is only because the cost has been too high and the road too long to lose us on the homestretch.

Upon what do you base your assurance of salvation? Does your assurance take into account the teachings of Jesus as a whole?

Fruit

Matthew 7:15-20

THE CHURCH YOU ATTEND is comprised of precious people very much like those who congregated on the mount where Jesus delivered his most famous sermon. In the crowd that day were spiritual babes who craved the pure milk of God's word, reeds bruised by the cruelties of life, salt-of-the-earth saints bearing the scars of organized religion, and open-minded seekers with eternity in their hearts. There is something about such an eclectic blend of people, united by their common attraction to Jesus, that feels like the kingdom of God—a safe place, surely.

To the contrary, this radically inclusive community is where predators lurk. "Watch out for false prophets," Jesus warned his precious flock. "They come to you in sheep's clothing, but inwardly they are ferocious wolves" (Matthew 7:15). They are masters of wooly disguise, never baring their glistening fangs, only seducing the unsuspecting faithful with faux piety, familiar jargon and irresistible passion. How can ordinary sheep like us ever hope to detect their sinister intentions?

"By their fruit you will recognize them," Jesus said. "Do people pick grapes from thornbushes, or figs from thistles? Likewise, every good tree bears good fruit, but a bad tree bears bad fruit. A good tree cannot bear bad fruit, and a bad tree cannot bear good fruit" (Matthew 7:16-18). Ah, so the heart of a teacher, invisible as it is, cannot but reveal itself! False prophets always produce bad fruit—which we interpret almost instinctively to mean bad behavior. If their life and the lives of their devotees are good (as tricky as that can be to discern), they can be trusted, right?

But then why did Jesus, when he condemned the *fruit* of the Pharisees, ask them, "How can you who are evil *say* anything good?" (Matthew 12:34a). And why did he say to them, "The mouth *speaks* what the heart is full of" (Matthew 12:34b)? And why did he say, "By your *words* you will be acquitted, and by your *words* you will be condemned" (Matthew 12:37)? Perhaps we are looking for fruit in all the wrong places, trying to diagnose the heart condition of our teachers by inspecting whatever parts of their life they choose to show us, when their very words betray them.

Do they, like the thornbushes of Jesus' day, offer a steep stairway to heaven constructed of a thousand grueling steps? Or do they, like so many thistles in our day, edit out the unmarketable aspects of discipleship until all that is left is inspirational fuel for me-worship? Whether the teachings of false prophets advocate legalism or license, they do not quote, promote or echo Jesus. Their fruit is bad, and so is their future. "Every tree that does not bear good fruit is cut down and thrown into the fire" (Matthew 7:19).

If you do not want to fall under their spell, or share their fate, feast on the good fruit of Jesus. A palate that has been refined to savor his teachings will reject all else as junk food.

What bad fruit are you most vulnerable to ingesting? What has Jesus said to help you know it is bad?

Lordship

LUKE 6:46

"Why do you call me, 'Lord, Lord,' and do not do what I say?" (Luke 6:46). How could anyone with self-awareness not be leveled by these words of Jesus? For, though we love him passionately and trust him implicitly, is not the evidence irrefutable that our obedience to him is incomplete?

After all, has the eye of lust been gouged out? Has the hand of adultery been cut off? We hunger and thirst for righteousness, yes, but are we pure in heart, or do we still see and touch what we know we should not?

When we are wounded unmercifully, do we now turn the other cheek, or is it still eye for eye and tooth for tooth? When someone takes what belongs to us, do we demand it back or insist on giving more? Do we love our enemies? Are we kind to the ungrateful and wicked? Do we pray for the good of those who persecute us? Can we honestly say that we do to others what we wish they would do to us? Does the light of our good deeds shine so brightly that others cannot help but give glory to our Father in heaven?

How much more discreet has our piety become? When we give to those in need, do we trumpet our generosity or hide from our left hand what our right hand is doing? When we pray, do we do it on street corners or behind closed doors? When we fast, do we wash our face or disfigure it?

Have we embraced poverty and hunger, or are we still rich and well-fed? Is our heart still on earth or has it relocated to heaven? Do we serve God or money? Which are we seeking first—God's kingdom or our provision?

How mercifully do we measure the failings of others? Are we as forgiving of their specks as we are of our own planks?

It is one thing to admire the Sermon on the Mount, but how many of us fully obey it? Do we dare admit that we are among those whose righteousness does not surpass that of the Pharisees and teachers of the law? Will we concede that we do indeed set aside the least of Christ's commands? Can we acknowledge that we are not perfect, as our heavenly Father is perfect?

We must, because this is where grace hides. The kingdom of heaven belongs to the poor in spirit. Do you see Jesus on the cross? For whom did he die, if not for those of us who call him Lord, Lord yet do not do what he says?

Which verse in the Sermon on the Mount most clearly exposes your need for grace?

Obedience

Matthew 7:21

IT FEELS RATHER SAFE to admit that we call Jesus Lord but not to do what he says because, thank God, where sin abounds, grace abounds all the more. What is the Sermon on the Mount if not an exposé on our true condition that makes the message of the cross the best news ever?

But then why did Jesus say, "Not everyone who says to me, 'Lord, Lord,' will enter the kingdom of heaven, but only the one who does the will of my Father who is in heaven" (Matthew 7:21)? Could it be that the quest for righteousness does not end at the cross but rather begins there? Could it be that this sermon was preached by our Lord not only to aid us in self-diagnosis, but also to describe the will of his Father in heaven for the rest of our life? And could it be that failure to hold to Christ's teachings, not only here but wherever we encounter them in Scripture, is a telltale symptom of rocky-soil faith?

Yes, clearly. How could grace have blinded us to it? But it is one thing to acknowledge the abstract truth that obedience to Jesus is mandatory, and it is something else altogether to ponder its implications line-by-line.

- "Blessed are those who are persecuted because of righteousness, for theirs is the kingdom of heaven" (Matthew 5:10).

- "It is better for you to lose one part of your body than for your whole body to go into hell" (Matthew 5:30).
- "Do not resist an evil person" (Matthew 5:39).
- "Love your enemies and pray for those who persecute you" (Matthew 5:44).
- "Be careful not to practice your righteousness in front of others to be seen by them" (Matthew 6:1).
- "Do not store up for yourselves treasures on earth" (Matthew 6:19).
- "Seek first his kingdom and his righteousness, and all these things will be given to you as well" (Matthew 6:33).
- "Do not judge" (Matthew 7:1).
- "Ask and it will be given to you" (Matthew 7:7).
- "In everything, do to others what you would have them do to you" (Matthew 7:12).

Now that we know we must put these words into practice, can we ever read them again without feeling tremors under our feet?

Even the most well-worn Bible has pages white with avoidance. What red-letter passage do you evade most vigilantly? Your spirit knows that you cannot do so forever. For not everyone who says to Jesus, "Lord, Lord," will enter the kingdom of heaven, but only those who do the will of his Father who is in heaven. The day will come—indeed, it must come—when you will, in fear and trembling, abandon yourself to radical obedience.

Oh, what joy, what freedom, awaits! For it is in the doing of what we find most daunting that Christ's yoke proves to be as easy, and his burden as light, as he promised.

What, in your life, is the unfulfilled will of God?

Miracles

MATTHEW 7:22-23

LIVING AS WE DO ON THE CUSP OF ETERNITY, with a river of delights flowing above and a lake of flames raging below, we cannot help but seek assurances that we are destined for the new Jerusalem rather than the second death. And if we shiver at the thought that only those who do the will of God will be welcomed home by him, we may fill in obedience gaps with miracle stories, be they few or many, for how could we whom God has used so powerfully not be heaven-bound?

Even if we do not claim to be prophets, we have at times sensed that Jesus used our voice to speak his words—gently, like light from a lamp or milk from a mother's breast, or powerfully, as if our words were like a fire, a hammer, a sword. How thrilling it is to be a spokesperson for the Lord!

Or we have found ourselves in spiritual battles as bloody as any military conflict, facing foes more fierce than soldiers. Though the power we encountered was beyond our strength, we watched the omnipotent authority of Christ subdue demonic spirits, and now we have spine-shivering war stories to tell.

And though we are reluctant to regale others with our most incredible moments of ministry, we may well have seen people healed with a touch—our touch! God has answered our prayers in ways that cannot be dismissed as coincidences.

Surely, Lord, these amazing things we have done in your name will authenticate our faith on the Day of Judgment.

No.

"Many will say to me on that day, 'Lord, Lord, did we not prophesy in your name and in your name drive out demons and in your name perform many miracles?' Then I will tell them plainly, 'I never knew you. Away from me, you evildoers!'" (Matthew 7:22-23).

How shocking that prophetic words can be uttered, evil spirits can be exorcised, and miracles can be performed in Jesus' name by those he does not know.

If we want to feel secure about our eternal destiny, we dare not trust in our ministry resumé. Rather, let us ask ourselves if we know Jesus, and he knows us. Where do we find the answer to that question? John, the disciple whom Jesus loved and who sat near him on the Mount, listened well that day, for six decades later he was still echoing what Jesus said: "We know that we have come to know him if we keep his commands" (1 John 2:3).

No miracle verifies our faith. Only obedience does. Have you done the will of your Father in heaven? Have you been, not just a hearer of these words of Jesus, but a doer of them? If so, whether the spirits submit to you or not, you can rejoice that your name is written in heaven.

What must you do to prioritize obedience over ministry?

Foundation

MATTHEW 7:24-27

THE WORD OF GOD that was spoken by Jesus that day so long ago is still alive and active today, judging the thoughts and attitudes of our heart. What has it revealed about you?

Have you decided that this sermon is the foundation upon which you want to build your life? Are you willing to adopt poverty of spirit as a lifelong posture, endlessly confessing how far you fall short of the ideal to which Jesus pointed? Do you want him to tinker with, or even overhaul, what you believe most stubbornly? Are you prepared to swim against the current for the rest of your life, eschewing earthly attractions and accomplishments for the all-in gamble that Jesus was right and the rest of the world wrong? Do you have the wherewithal to build such an out-of-place edifice despite the snickers and pity of your neighbors, your colleagues, your family—perhaps even your most religious friends?

Or have you concluded that the words of Jesus, though poetic and pithy, are utterly impractical? For who really believes that poverty is preferable to wealth or that meekness yields a better return than assertiveness? How can anyone live with the guilt trip that Jesus put on people who have done nothing worse than seethe or fantasize? Isn't it unrealistic to invite a second punch to the face, to pay twice what a plaintiff demands, to give whatever anyone wants and never ask for it back? Who actually responds to hatred with love and prays for God's blessing on their persecutors? What kind of financial advisor would recommend investing in life-after-death treasures rather than a 401(k)? As expensive and unpredictable as life is, and as elusive as God can be, is it prudent to rivet your focus on advancing his kingdom and expect him to give you what you need when you need it? And, as commendable as kindness is, how can we be expected to do for others what we'd like them to do for us every single time?

Oh, how the words of Jesus penetrate, sometimes dividing even the cautious soul and daring spirit in a single conflicted listener.

It is to both the adventurous and the risk-averse that Jesus says: "Everyone who hears these words of mine and puts them into practice is like a wise man who built his house on the rock. The rain came down, the streams rose, and the winds blew and beat against that house; yet it did not fall, because it had its foundation on the rock. But everyone who hears these words of mine and does not put them into practice is like a foolish man who built his house on sand. The rain came down, the streams rose, and the winds blew and beat against that house, and it fell with a great crash" (Matthew 7:24-27).

Yes, there is risk to be weighed—but who is in danger? Not the one who trembles at Jesus' words yet resolves to obey them, but the one who hears his voice and walks away unchanged. When the rain comes down, when the streams rise, when the winds blow and beat against the house you have built, it will stand only if the Sermon on the Mount has been to you, not a song to be enjoyed or a threat to be avoided, but the manifesto that, from this day forward, will shape the days and years of your life.

Are you betting your life that Jesus was right or wrong in what he taught in the Sermon on the Mount? What would others say based on your lifestyle?

If we have practiced the discipline of slowness in our study of the Sermon on the Mount, if we have gone beyond mere comprehension, meditating on the teachings of Jesus until their implications emerge through our jungle of distractions, surely we have learned that every word that proceeds from his mouth is revolutionary. Does not the thought that we have only scratched the surface take your breath away?

What if you were to linger over every Christ-quote preserved for you in Scripture as if wandering through a museum full of masterpieces with a lifetime pass in your pocket? How thoroughly would your mind be renewed? How dramatically would your life be transformed?

Already you feel the urge to recalibrate your pace with this world in which it is always rush hour. Resist the temptation to keep up with the Marthas, and sit at the feet of Jesus, listening "like a lily that is lifting its chalice to the sun" (R.C.H. Lenski). This is where Life begins.

If this book has been spiritually beneficial to you, would you be willing to help more readers find it by writing a customer review on Amazon and/or recommending it to others with a picture of the book and your endorsement on social media? As an independent author, I am grateful for your partnership. Thank you.

GS

Made in the USA
Columbia, SC
21 June 2022